THE REAL RANKING OF THE PRESIDENTS

An Accomplishments-Based Evaluation

Terry L. Koglin

DORRANCE
PUBLISHING CO
EST. 1920
PITTSBURGH, PENNSYLVANIA 15238

Dorrance Publishing Co
585 Alpha Drive
Pittsburgh, PA 15238
Visit our website at *www.dorrancebookstore.com*

ISBN: 978-1-6480-4944-6
eISBN: 978-1-6480-4538-7

CONTENTS

ACKNOWLEDGMENTS

The author wishes to thank A. Donald Seep, James Stephenson, and particularly Dennis J. Marchetti for adding their wisdom to this project. All opinions stated and facts presented are the sole responsibility of the author.

Additional thanks are due to National Cable Satellite Corporation (C-SPAN), Professor Iwan Morgan, Kensington Publishing Company, Siena Research Institute, Penn State University Press, The Independent Institute, and the American Political Science Association, for allowing their materials to be cited in this book. It is hoped that others, who did not respond to our requests, did so because of the age of the material or because it was tacitly considered to be in the public domain. The efforts of all of the creators of the prior studies cited in this work are appreciated.

INTRODUCTION

The United States is one of the few federal republics in the world. A federal republic is created by a grouping of sovereign states that give up part of their sovereignty to a central administration. Each federal republic has its own rules as to what part of sovereignty is held by the central power and what part is retained by its constituent states. The original thirteen states that made up the United States, having had serious difficulties after achieving independence in 1781, revised how their federal republic would function by ratifying the Constitution, which is the book of rules for the federal government. Per the Constitution, in the United States, each state has two members in the Senate, in spite of the smallest state, Rhode Island, having less than one-half of one percent of the area of the largest, Alaska, and the state with the least population, Wyoming, having less than two percent of the population of the state with the largest population, California. In the House of Representatives, where membership is based on population, each state is guaranteed at least one vote in spite of its population (as it happens, even the least populated state as of the 2010 Census, Wyoming, has a sufficient number of residents to entitle it to one Representative based on its share of the total population of the United States). In choosing the president, each state has power equal to the sum of its House and Senate representation.

The basic rule of operation for the Government of the United States, the Constitution of the United States of America, has been amended several times since its adoption in 1788. It defines the office of the president, and provides rules on the selection of the person who is to fill that office. The preamble to the Constitution states: "We the People of the United States, in Order to form a more perfect Union, establish Justice, insure domestic Tranquility, provide for the common defence (sic), promote the general Welfare, and secure the Blessings of Liberty to ourselves and our Posterity, do ordain and establish this CONSTITUTION for the United States of America." The Founding Fathers believed that Congress, the legislature, would be the heart of the government, and most of the details of what the United States government could do and not do, were described in the section, Article I, describing Congress.

The President was looked upon as an administrator, with one of his primary duties being to "take care that the laws be faithfully executed." These laws are made by Congress, with the president's only direct input being to veto laws he believes to be inappropriate. Even this input can be overridden by Congress, if they can muster enough votes in the House of Representatives and the Senate. According to the Constitution, the President is also head of state, a sort of elected King. The history of countries with elected kings is not very good: Poland, for one, ended up being partitioned out of existence by its neighbors Prussia, Russia, and Austria, and the Holy Roman Emperor was largely impotent in the empire's later existence due to its member states becoming overly strong, and the Emperor became largely a figurehead.

The Constitution details specific tasks to be performed by the president; these can be briefly described as: Head of State, Commander in Chief, and Executor of the Laws. Further detail of these duties, per the Constitution, are as follows:

Head of State
    Make Treaties
    Appoint Ambassadors
    Receive Ambassadors

Commander in Chief
    Head of the Army
    Head of the Navy
    Head of the Militia when serving the United States
    Commission all Officers of the United States

Executor of the Laws
    Require Opinions of Heads of Departments

Grant Reprieves and Pardons
Appoint Justices of the Supreme Court
Appoint Other Officers Not Otherwise Provided For
Give Congress Information on the State of the Union
Give Recommendations to Congress on Necessary Measures
Convene Congress on Extraordinary Occasions
Adjourn Congress when House and Senate Cannot Agree on Adjournment
See to it that the Laws are Faithfully Executed

In addition, the president has the following powers per the Constitution:
Veto laws of Congress, subject to conditions of override
Guarantee to each State a Republican form of Government
Protect each State against invasion
Protect each State against domestic Violence, when requested

No additional powers have been granted to the president by any constitutional amendments, except where Congress has been given authority to enact additional legislation, which the president is then required to enforce.

In order to assist the president in performance of his duties, several cabinet departments have been created, some per specific constitutional requirements, and others in order to comply with Acts of Congress. There have been additions, rearrangements, consolidations, and eliminations to the cabinet. At present, it is composed of the following positions, in approximate chronological order of establishment:

Secretary of State
Secretary of the Treasury
Attorney General
Secretary of the Interior
Secretary of Agriculture
Secretary of Commerce
Secretary of Labor
Secretary of Defense (replaced much earlier War and Navy secretaries)
Secretary of Housing and Urban Development
Secretary of Transportation

Secretary of Energy
Secretary of Health and Human Services
Secretary of Education
Secretary of Veterans Affairs
Secretary of Homeland Security

Several of the above secretaries are heads of departments covering activities not specifically mentioned in the Constitution. In addition, there are many federal agencies not part of any of the above departments, but for which the president is nominally responsible. These extraconstitutional responsibilities are generally considered to be implied powers under the necessary and proper clause of Section 8 of Article I of the Constitution. In addition, many presidents have performed deeds that do not relate to any of the above. Some of these deeds have taken the form of "executive orders," in which the president unilaterally makes a rule and then enforces it. Debate over the legality of these extraconstitutional duties helps justify the existence of various libertarian parties, and the "strict constructionist" view of the United States Government held by many political conservatives.

Election to the Presidency of the United States by the Electoral College is based on a combination of state sovereignty and population, with each state guaranteed at least three votes, but with additional votes allocated to states according to their population. Thus, per the 2010 Census, California has 55 electoral votes while Alaska, Delaware, Montana, North Dakota, South Dakota, Vermont, and Wyoming have only three electoral votes. After almost every presidential election, the losing side complains about the unfairness of the Electoral College. The Democrats or their predecessors have lost 30 presidential elections and the Republicans or their predecessors have lost 28 presidential elections, so the results are fairly even. If only two-person presidential races are considered, the Democrats do have grounds for complaint, as Republicans John Quincy Adams in 1824, Rutherford B. Hayes in 1876, Benjamin Harrison in 1888, George W. Bush in 2000, and Donald Trump in 2016 all won the election while polling fewer popular votes than their opponents (see Appendix B).

It must be said, however, that in some of these elections minor candidates who were aligned ideologically with the winner kept the losing Democrat from getting an absolute majority of the popular vote. This was the case in the two most contentious cases, the election of 1824 and the election of 2016 (see Appendix B). The loser in 1824, Andrew Jackson, and the loser in 2016, Hilary Clinton, with their adherents, argued loud and long and made the winners' presidencies very difficult, but did not have a valid case for complaint. If in a parliamentary system of government, it is likely the winner or "prime minister" would have been the same person as the one who ended up president. The constitutional rules for choosing the president were not intended by the original framers of the Constitution to be purely democratic, and none of the subsequent amendments to the Constitution except for Number 15, Number 19, Number 22, Number 23, Number 24, and Number 26 have resulted in a material change to the degree of democratic nature of the method of choosing the president.

In another example of federalism in the United States, the Constitution, including the means of electing the president, can only be changed by the States, without consideration of population, and three-quarters of the states must agree to the change. Any change in the rules for electing the president is unlikely, as only a little over half the states are "red," or Republican-leaning, resulting in something like a 50-50 split on any partisan question. While less than one-quarter of the states are "blue," or strongly Democrat-leaning, there are several "purple" states, so that the blue percentage approaches 30%, with several purple states that are likely to join the blue states in preventing a change in the rules to favor red-state politics.

The most common complaint is that the president should be selected only by population, throwing out the Electoral College. There is some validity to this, as only 16 of the states were actually once independent countries or colonies: Delaware, Pennsylvania, New Jersey, Georgia, Connecticut, Massachusetts, Maryland, South Carolina, New Hampshire, Virginia, New York, North Carolina, and Rhode Island (the original thirteen) and Texas, California, and Hawaii. A few other states experienced some quasi-independence, but never established themselves as bona fide independent countries. Thirty-four states are actually creations of the federal government, so could be considered as subservient to it. It is questionable whether this change would actually make any difference in the selection, as the Red State and Blue/Purple State populations are fairly equal, and only a handful of presidential elections have had a winner who did not get a plurality of the popular vote, and these were usually very close in the popular vote. The major exception is the election of 1824, in which the winner, John Quincy Adams, got only 31.80% of the popular vote, while one of the losers, Andrew Jackson, got 42.60% of the popular vote. Adams and his ally, Henry Clay, got a total of 45 percent of the popular vote, but Jackson ignored this fact while crying foul (history repeats itself; Hilary Clinton and her Democratic Party colleagues did the same thing after the 2016 election even though Trump and his political cohorts (Johnson and McMullin) got 50.20% of the popular vote). As no candidate obtained a majority of the electoral vote in the 1824 election, the House of Representatives, following the Constitution, chose Adams. Jackson and his followers, although they had no valid cause, were quite irate, and remained so until Jackson eventually won, in 1828.

Originally, the Constitution did not consider the existence of political parties. George Washington considered political parties to be pernicious and a detriment to good government. In the election of president and vice president, the Constitution originally called for collection of electoral votes from each state, with the person winning the most votes becoming president, provided he had a majority of the total number of votes cast, with the person coming in second becoming vice president. After the election of 1800, when two leading candidates received the same number of electoral votes, forcing the House of Representatives to choose the president, the 12th Amendment was ratified in 1804, so that the president and vice president ran on the same ticket, thus implying the existence of political parties. Since then the House has only had to choose the president once, in 1824, when several prominent candidates ran as independents. No further Constitutional change to the means of electing the president has been made other than preventing restrictions on ex-slaves voting, in 1870 (15th Amendment), giving the right to vote to women, in 1920 (19th Amendment), limiting the number of terms a president can serve, in 1951 (22nd Amendment), giving three electoral votes to the District of Columbia, in 1961 (23rd Amendment), eliminating the poll tax, in 1964 (24th Amendment), and lowering the voting age to 18, in 1971 (26th Amendment). In a definitive nod to federalism, in the case of no candidate receiving a majority of the electoral vote, the House of Representatives chooses the president, with each *state* having one vote, regardless of population or number of Representatives in Congress.

In the history of the United States, since the beginning of government under the Constitution in 1789 to 2020 (see Appendix C), the government, including both houses of Congress and the Presidency, has been controlled by the Democrats, or their predecessors, 35.3 percent of the time, while they have controlled the presidency 48.5 percent of the time (50.2% if John Quincy Adams is included). The Republicans have controlled the government 22.5 percent of the time while controlling the presidency 49.8 percent of the time (51.5% if John Quincy Adams is included). John Tyler and Andrew Johnson are considered Republicans for the purposes of this evaluation, although their party loyalty is questionable or nonexistent. The federal government has been divided 42.2 percent of the time, with one party controlling the presidency and the other party controlling one or both houses of Congress. In actuality, there have been five distinct periods in the history of the United States when one party, or no party, has been dominant. From 1789 to 1801 the Federalists (read modern-day Republicans) controlled the government 50 percent of the time while ancestors of the present-day Democrats never controlled the government, as it was divided for the remainder of the period. From 1789 to 1801 only Federalists (assuming Washington was a Federalist) sat in the presidency. From 1801 to 1861, the Democrats or their predecessors have controlled the government 73 percent of the time, and held the presidency 80 percent of the time. From 1861 to 1933, the Republicans controlled the government 52.8 percent of the time while holding the presidency 75 percent of the time. From 1933 to 1981 the Democrats controlled the government 62.5 percent of the time while having a president in office 66.7 percent of the time. From 1981 to 2019, the government was mixed, or divided, 75 percent of the time, while the Republicans held the presidency 60 percent of the time. This cyclic nature of American politics can have several explanations.

Several presidents have had the luxury of holding office for their entire term or terms with a sympathetic congress. These include John Adams, Thomas Jefferson, James Madison, James Monroe, Andrew Jackson, Martin Van Buren, Abraham Lincoln, William McKinley, Theodore Roosevelt, Warren Harding, Calvin Coolidge, Franklin Roosevelt, John F. Kennedy, Lyndon Johnson, and Jimmy Carter. This has not necessarily been helpful in securing them entry to the pantheon of the greatest presidents. Only one of these presidents, Abraham Lincoln, is universally recognized as one of our very greatest presidents. Two others, Thomas Jefferson and Theodore Roosevelt, are held in high esteem by most authorities. All the others are rated highly or not so high depending on who is doing the evaluation.

CHAPTER 1 — THE PRESIDENTS

This book was originally intended as an unbiased, factual evaluation of each of the 45 presidents of the United States. It soon became apparent that results were not equal. Of the three best, or "great" presidents, all were Republicans or, in the case of George Washington, non-party but leaning strongly to the Federalists, who were the "grandfathers" of the modern-day Republicans. Of the four "very good" presidents, two were Democrats or their early equivalent and two were Republicans or Federalists. Of the thirteen "better-than-average" presidents, twelve were Republicans and only one was a Democrat; and that was James Monroe, who was elected essentially unopposed, as no opposition party existed, and the "Democrats" (called "Republicans") at that time soon split into two opposing parties, the National Republicans under Henry Clay, represented by John Quincy Adams, and the Democratic Republicans, led by Andrew Jackson.

At the other end of the scale, the four "bad" presidents were Pierce, Buchanan, Jackson, and Lyndon Johnson, and the four "poor" presidents were Obama, Wilson, Madison, and Kennedy. All eight of these presidents were officially Democrats, except for James Madison, who was a member of the party that eventually became the Democrats.

In the middle are presidents who registered as non-entities: Benjamin Harrison, William Henry Harrison, and James A. Garfield, plus Grover Cleveland in his first administration, plus Donald Trump who is not evaluated as his presidency is still in progress as of April, 2020. Twenty-five presidents, more than half of the total, are ranked either slightly above or slightly below average. All but one of the slightly above average presidents are Republicans, eight of the twelve slightly below average presidents are Democrats although two, John Tyler and Andrew Johnson, were elected as vice presidents on Republican or Whig (pre-modern-day-Republican) tickets, and succeeded to the presidency on the death of the ticket leaders.

Summarizing, in a feat of near mirror imagery, seventeen of the twenty-two best presidents were Republicans (or members of predecessor parties), while sixteen of the twenty-two worst presidents were Democrats (or members of predecessor parties). This is not a coincidence. The present-day Democratic Party grew out of the 18th-Century Antifederalist party, which opposed ratification of the Constitution, while the present-day Republican Party grew out of the 18th-Century Federalist Party, which supported ratification of the Constitution. It is true that a reversal of roles took place over the middle decades of the 20th Century as the Democrats abandoned their states-rights policy and the Republicans gradually embraced it, calling it "federalism." This temporary reversal passed, and the principles that guided the members of the Constitutional Convention are largely those of the present-day Republican Party, while the present-day Democrats mostly favor what could be interpreted as creative interpretation of the Constitution, but is actually, harking to their Antifederalist forebears, a desire to ignore the Constitution. For example, Democrats continually attempt to pass laws restricting the right of citizens to own weapons, and have succeeded in obtaining Supreme Court decisions reducing the right to bear arms to ownership of sporting weapons. Republicans, on the other hand, consistently maintain that the 2nd Amendment is absolute. Fascist and communist police states are the most adamant about refusing to allow the populace to possess weapons; nations that most value individual freedom invariably rely on citizen armies for defense. Regarding the 1st Amendment, Republicans generally take the freedom of press, religion, assembly, and petition literally, while Democrats tend to prefer a popular vote on each issue, as long as the result agrees with their position.

There are some significant changes in the operation of the federal government that are not the result of constitutional amendments. The members of the Constitutional Convention assumed that Congress would be the heart of the government, making laws and having various powers. The President was assumed to be primarily an administrator of laws passed by Congress, and was to be assisted in his role as head of state by the Senate. The people developed less and less respect for Congress over the years, until today only the press is held in lower esteem by the public than is Congress. This does not, however, keep most members of Congress from easily getting reelected. The President, because he is the representative of all the people, is increasingly looked at as the leader and director of both domestic and foreign policy. Exceptions to this occur occasionally when an extremely unpopular president occupies the office.

The Constitution does not specify how the constitutionality of laws is to be determined. The Supreme Court gradually took over that duty, and is now generally acknowledged to be the ultimate authority on the subject. This has increased the power of the President significantly, as that office has sole power of nominating prospective members to the Supreme Court, subject to confirmation by the Senate.

The original political concept for the United States was for a governing committee representing all interests, making decisions based on consensus. While this worked at the beginning, as the Second Continental Congress expanded into just "Congress," or more formally, "The United States in Congress Assembled," there were definitely shortcomings. Material support for George Washington's Continental Army was very, very slow in coming, and the various state militias were extremely slow in responding to crises, if they responded at all. It is extremely unlikely that the United States would have survived if France had not, after the British self-inflicted debacle at Saratoga, stepped in with full, open support of the revolutionaries.

After the Treaty of Paris, it soon became obvious to all thoughtful Americans that the loose union established in North America under the Articles of Confederation was inadequate for the needs of the new country. Conflicts and jealousies between states, with no path to resolution, lack of respect internationally, and inadequate means of funding the requirements of Congress, made it evident that a major change had to be made.

Congress took the bold step of establishing a convention of delegates from each of the thirteen essentially independent states that formed the confederacy called the United States. The difficulty of the project was quickly made apparent with the slowness of delegates to appear. Rhode Island never sent any delegates, and the recall by New York of its delegates (although Alexander Hamilton stayed on, on his own dime) ended their official presence. On top of that, the convention went beyond its mandate by throwing out the Articles of Confederation, rather than revising them, and proposing an entirely new

Constitution that went beyond the federal nature of the Articles and interjected new nationalistic concepts into their proposed form of government.

The Constitutional Convention was marked by strenuous, spirited debate over several issues, but it soon became apparent that there were two splits in the delegation, both potentially fatal to the process. The first to become apparent was the big state – small state divide. All the small states, which meant all except Virginia, Pennsylvania, and Massachusetts, were perfectly happy with all decisions being made by state votes, each state being equal. The large states, led by Virginia, thought that their larger contribution to the wealth of the country entitled them to a larger share in the decision-making process. John Randolph, delegate from Virginia, proposed in detail a truly national government, in which the states would have a minor role in government, and might perhaps be eliminated altogether. His plan called for a national assembly that would represent the people, with representation based on population. The smaller states, led by Connecticut and New Jersey in particular, refused absolutely to give up their equal status. Eventually a compromise was reached, whereby each state would have equal representation in the Senate, which would have a larger role in the government than the House of Representatives, in which each state would have a delegation the size of which would be based on population.

Today, the 12 largest states have 283 electoral votes, substantially more than half, so that they can control the House of Representatives (with 259 of 435 Representatives) and the Presidency, while the 38 small states (39 including the District of Columbia when adding electoral votes) can control the Senate with 76 of 100 votes. Based on the 2016 election, the large states are split, however, with 132 conservative electoral votes and 118 liberal electoral votes, plus 33 neutral votes, so that any given presidential election could go in any direction within these states. The 38 small states are also split, but are more biased to the conservative side, with 153 conservative electoral votes and only 66 (69 including the District of Columbia) liberal electoral votes, with 33 neutral or purple votes (see tables). The tendency of certain large and small states is to agree on a conservative bias, with 285 electoral votes. The small and large liberal states only can muster 184 electoral votes; even if they win over all seven neutral states, with 66 electoral votes, they are still, adding the District of Columbia's three votes, in the minority with 253 electoral votes in a presidential contest that requires 538/2+1=270 electoral votes to win. Neither the large or small states can win on any issue without their liberal and conservative factions joining forces; in addition the thirty-nine small states would need to add Virginia and New Jersey to their ranks to win a majority of electoral votes.

A larger split at the Constitutional Convention developed over slavery. The southern slave states refused to allow any restriction or aspersions on slavery to be entered into the Constitution, and some delegates from northern states refused to sign any document that did not put restrictions on slavery. Eventually a compromise was reached that largely gave the game to the southerners, even banning export taxes which would have largely fallen on the southern, or "staple producing" slave states. Northerners generally conceded due to the realization that economic viability of the new country would be seriously compromised without the rice and tobacco exports of the south if Maryland, Virginia, North and South Carolina, and Georgia were to refuse to join the union. Cotton was not an important export commodity until the invention of the cotton gin, after the Constitution was ratified. Cotton then became "king," further increasing the political leverage of the southern slave states. The slavery split, of course, became obsolete with the Northern victory in the Civil War and the passage of the 13th Amendment to the Constitution, outlawing slavery.

And so agreement was reached on a new Constitution. It was understood by all that Congress would be the heart of the new government, with a President responsible for carrying out and enforcing laws passed by Congress, and answerable to it by being subject to impeachment. Congress, on the other hand, was to be untouchable, with neither the President nor the courts able to deny the right of Congress to do as it wished. Later presidents would be able to provide some leadership to Congress, but this was only informal and dependent on the stature of the particular president. In the Constitution, the Supreme Court was not given the explicit authority to reject acts of Congress as unconstitutional, but eventually took this responsibility and was finally sustained on all sides in its assumption of the task.

There were many questions on government procedure, including determination of constitutionality, that were not answered within the Constitution, and most of these were worked out in the first years after ratification.

The major philosophical split at the federal level today is a conflict between conservatives and liberals. It can be expressed as a rural versus urban conflict. See Figure 1-1, below:

PRES VOTE 2016   AS OF DECEMBER 2017

PRES VOTE 2016

STATE	VOTES	MAJOR CANDIDATES TRUMP	CLINTON	JOHNSON	STEIN	MCMULLIN	IN A "2 PARTY" SYSTEM: "REP" T+J+McM	"DEM" C+S	"W"	PERCENT CONSERV	##	POPULATION	RED VS BLUE	CUMULATIVE ELECTORAL VOTE
1 WY	3	174,248	55,949	13,285	2,512		187,533	58,461	T	76.23%	##	RURAL	RED	3
2 WV	5	486,198	187,457	22,798	8,000		508,996	195,457	T	72.25%	##	RURAL	RED	8
3 UT	6	397,004	237,241	27,735	6,072	175,301	600,040	243,313	T	71.15%	##	URBAN	RED	14
4 OK	7	947,934	419,788	83,334	0		1,031,268	419,788	T	71.07%	##	RURAL	RED	21
5 ND	3	216,133	93,526	21,351	3,769		237,484	97,295	T	70.94%	##	RURAL	RED	24
6 ID	4	407,199	189,677	28,256	8,464	46,538	481,993	198,141	T	70.87%	##	RURAL	RED	28
7 SD	3	227,701	117,442	20,845	0		248,546	117,442	T	67.91%	##	RURAL	RED	31
8 KY	8	1,202,942	628,834	53,749	13,913	22,780	1,279,471	642,747	T	66.56%	##	RURAL	RED	39
9 AL	9	1,306,925	718,084	43,869	9,287		1,350,794	727,371	T	65.00%	##	RURAL	RED	48
10 NE	5	485,819	273,858	37,615	8,346		523,434	282,204	T	64.97%	##		URBAN RED	53
11 AR	6	677,904	378,729	29,518	9,837	13,069	720,491	388,566	T	64.96%	##	RURAL	RED	59
12 TN	11	1,517,402	867,110	70,084	15,919		1,587,486	883,029	T	64.26%	##	RURAL	RED	70
13 MT	3	274,120	174,521	27,264	7,669		301,384	182,190	T	62.32%	##	RURAL	PINK	73
14 IN	11	1,556,220	1,031,953	133,856	0		1,690,076	1,031,953	T	62.09%	##	RURAL	RED	84
15 KS	6	656,009	414,788	53,648	22,698		709,657	437,486	T	61.86%	##		URBAN RED	90
16 MO	10	1,585,753	1,054,889	96,404	25,086		1,682,157	1,079,975	T	60.90%	##	RURAL	RED	100
17 LA	8	1,178,004	779,535	37,950	14,018	8,546	1,224,500	793,553	T	60.68%	##	RURAL	RED	108
18 AK	3	130,415	93,007	14,593	4,445		145,008	97,452	T	59.81%	##	RURAL	RED	111
19 MS	6	678,457	462,001	13,789	3,580		692,246	465,581	T	59.79%	##	RURAL	RED	117
20 SC	9	1,143,611	849,469	48,715	12,917	20,795	1,213,121	862,386	T	58.45%	##	RURAL	RED	126
21 IA	6	798,923	650,790	57,322	11,119	12,267	868,512	661,909	T	56.75%	##	RURAL	PINK	132
22 TX	38	4,681,590	3,867,816	282,524	71,307		4,964,114	3,939,123	T	55.76%	##		URBAN PINK	170
23 OH	18	2,771,984	2,317,001	168,599	44,310		2,940,583	2,361,311	T	55.46%	##	RURAL	PINK	188
24 GA	16	2,068,623	1,837,300	123,641	0		2,192,264	1,837,300	T	54.40%	##	RURAL	RED	204
25 AZ	11	1,017,166	933,655	79,874	25,195		1,097,040	958,850	T	53.36%	##		URBAN PINK	215
26 NC	15	2,339,603	2,162,074	127,794	0		2,467,397	2,162,074	T	53.30%	##	RURAL	PINK	230
27 WI	10	1,409,467	1,382,210	106,442	30,980		1,515,909	1,413,190	T	51.75%	##	RURAL	PINK	240
28 NH	4	345,598	348,126	30,530	6,374		376,128	354,500	T	51.48%	##	RURAL	PURPLE	244
29 MN	10	1,322,891	1,366,676	112,944	36,957	53,080	1,488,915	1,403,633	T	51.47%	##	RURAL	LAVENDER	254
30 MI	16	2,279,221	2,267,798	173,023	50,690		2,452,244	2,318,488	T	51.40%	##	RURAL	PURPLE	270
31 FL	29	4,605,515	4,485,745	206,007	64,019		4,811,522	4,549,764	T	51.40%	##		URBAN PINK	299
32 PA	20	2,912,941	2,844,705	142,653	48,912		3,055,594	2,893,617	T	51.36%	##	RURAL	PURPLE	319
33 CO	9	1,136,354	1,208,095	129,128	33,009	26,715	1,292,197	1,241,104	T	51.01%	##		URBAN LAVENDER	328
34 NV	6	511,319	537,753	37,299	0		548,618	537,753	T	50.50%	##		URBAN LAVENDER	334
35 NM	5	315,875	380,724	73,669	9,729	5,714	395,258	390,453	T	50.31%	##		URBAN LAVENDER	339
36 ME	4	334,838	354,873	37,764	14,075		372,602	368,948	T	50.25%	##	RURAL	PURPLE	343
37 VA	13	1,731,156	1,916,845	116,600	27,272	52,914	1,900,670	1,944,117	C	49.43%	##	RURAL	LAVENDER	
38 OR	7	742,506	934,631	86,306	45,132		828,812	979,763	C	45.83%	##		URBAN BLUE	
39 DE	3	185,103	235,581	14,751	6,100		199,854	241,681	C	45.26%	##	RURAL	BLUE	
40 CT	7	637,919	823,360	45,999	21,539		683,918	844,899	C	44.74%	##		URBAN BLUE	
41 NJ	14	1,535,513	2,021,755	68,695	35,949		1,604,208	2,057,704	C	43.81%	##	RURAL	LAVENDER	
42 IL	20	2,118,179	2,977,498	204,491	74,112		2,322,670	3,051,610	C	43.22%	##		URBAN BLUE	
43 RI	4	179,421	249,902	14,643	6,155		194,064	256,057	C	43.11%	##		URBAN BLUE	
44 WA	12	950,710	1,364,934	112,520	38,377		1,063,230	1,403,311	C	43.11%	##		URBAN BLUE	
45 NY	29	2,640,570	4,143,874	161,836	99,895		2,802,406	4,243,769	C	39.77%	##		URBAN BLUE	
46 MD	10	873,646	1,497,951	71,107	31,839		944,753	1,529,790	C	38.18%	##	RURAL	BLUE	
47 MA	11	1,083,069	1,964,768	136,784	46,910		1,219,853	2,011,678	C	37.75%	##		URBAN BLUE	
48 CA	55	3,021,095	5,589,936	288,310	155,706		3,309,405	5,745,642	C	36.55%	##		URBAN BLUE	
49 VT	3	95,050	178,117	10,043	6,745		105,093	184,862	C	36.24%	##	RURAL	BLUE	
50 HA	4	121,648	251,853	14,854	11,608		136,502	263,461	C	34.13%	##	RURAL	BLUE	
50X DC	3	11,553	260,223	4,501	3,995		16,054	264,218	C	5.73%	6%		URBAN BLUE	
TOTALS:		60,029,044	60,384,427	4,119,311	1,234,542	437,719	64,586,074	61,618,969		51.18%	##			

Figure 1-1 Percent Conservative Presidential Vote, by State, 2016

There are a few exceptions, but in the main, the "red" or conservative states have primarily rural populations, while the "blue" or liberal states are largely urban. In decreasing order of urban population, it looks like this, with Blue being most liberal, Lavender somewhat liberal, Purple non-committal, Pink somewhat conservative, and Red being most conservative (based on 2016 presidential election results, with some variation due to votes for third-party candidates):

STATE	ELECTORAL VOTES	% URBAN	% CONSERV- ATIVE	%URBAN- % CONS	POLITICAL STANCE
Arizona*	11	80.9	65.0	15.9	pink
California	55	80.8	37.0	43.8	blue
Nevada*	6	71.5	50.5	21.0	lavender
Rhode Island	4	70.4	43.1	27.3	blue
Utah*	6	69.3	71.2	-1.9	red
Massachusetts	11	66.7	37.8	28.9	blue
Colorado	9	65.7	51.0	14.7	lavender
Connecticut	7	65.1	44.7	20.4	blue
Texas	38	60.0	55.8	4.2	pink
New York	29	59.5	39.8	19.7	blue
Illinois	20	56.8	43.2	13.5	blue
New Mexico	5	53.2	50.3	2.9	lavender
Florida	29	50.9	51.4	-0.5	pink
Kansas	6	50.9	61.9	-11.0	red
Nebraska	5	50.3	65.0	-14.7	red
Oregon	7	50.1	45.8	4.3	blue
Washington	12	50.0	43.1	6.9	blue
Oklahoma	7	49.0	71.1	-22.1	red
Idaho	4	48.7	70.9	-22.2	red
Alaska	3	48.4	59.8	-11.4	red
North Dakota	3	47.8	70.9	-23.1	red
Minnesota	10	47.2	51.5	-4.3	lavender
Maryland	10	46.2	38.2	8.0	blue
Hawaii	4	46.0	34.1	11.9	blue
Indiana	11	45.1	62.1	-17.0	red
Tennessee	11	43.9	64.3	-20.4	red
Iowa	6	43.8	56.8	-13.0	pink
Wisconsin	10	40.8	51.8	-11.0	pink
N. Carolina	15	40.5	53.3	-12.8	pink
Virginia	13	39.1	49.4	-10.3	lavender
Ohio	18	38.9	55.5	-16.6	pink
Arkansas	6	37.1	65.0	-27.9	red
Missouri	10	36.6	60.9	-24.3	red
Michigan	16	34.7	51.4	-16.7	purple
Louisiana	8	34.0	60.7	-26.7	red
Montana	3	33.7	62.3	-29.6	pink
Alabama	9	33.2	65.0	-31.8	red
New Hampshire	4	33.1	51.5	-18.4	purple
South Dakota	3	32.2	67.9	-35.7	red
Wyoming	3	31.8	76.2	-44.4	red
Kentucky	8	31.1	66.6	-35.5	red
Georgia	16	29.1	54.4	-25.3	red
New Jersey	14	27.5	43.8	-16.3	lavender
Mississippi	6	22.9	59.8	-36.9	red
Pennsylvania	20	22.5	51.4	-28.9	purple
S. Carolina	9	20.4	58.5	-38.1	red
Delaware	3	14.8	45.3	-30.5	blue
Maine	4	12.0	50.3	-38.3	purple
West Virginia	5	10.1	72.3	-62.2	red
Vermont**	3	6.8	36.2	-29.4	blue

*states largely desert with very small truly rural populations
**Vermont is largely populated with transplanted or retired New Yorkers

Figure 1-2 Urban vs. Rural Population and Voting

As can be seen, of the seventeen states with an urban population of 50% or more, eleven, or 65%, are liberal; i.e. blue or lavender. Three are "desert" states with a nearly uninhabitable countryside; removing Arizona, Nevada, and Utah from the mix leaves 10 of 14 or 71% liberal. The other four red or pink states in the top seventeen, Texas, Florida, Kansas, and Nebraska, are hardly perceived as "urban." Of the 33 states with less than 50% urban population, 22, or 67%, are conservative, i.e. red or pink. Removing Vermont, largely a home for retired people from New York City, Delaware, a corporate haven, and New Jersey, also a corporate haven but essentially a continuation of New York City, from this list, makes 22/30, or 73%, conservative. By this standard, of the 21 states, less three, that are most rural (<40% urban), 13 of 18, or 72%, are conservative. All four neutral, or purple, states are rural, with less than 50% urban population. See the graph, Figure 1-3, for a visual rendition of the trend to decreasing conservatism with increasing urban population.

POLITICAL CONSERVATISM VS PERCENT URBAN, BY STATE

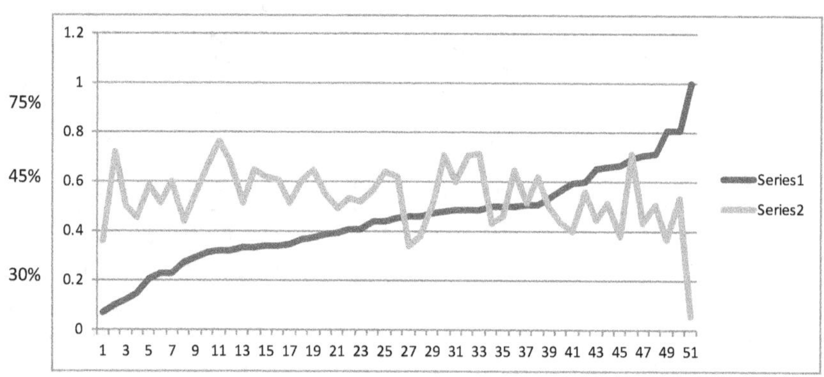

Figure 1-3 Urban versus Conservative Voting Population

CHAPTER 2 — THE DEMOCRAT PRESIDENTS

From Antifederalist through "Republican" (Jefferson style), Democratic Republican, and finally through Democrat, presidents and politicians in this group have consistently not been enamored of the Constitution. It is appropriate that the two presidents commonly considered the founders of the Democratic Party, Thomas Jefferson and Andrew Jackson, both considered the Constitution an impediment. Jefferson-Jackson Day dinners were once a high point in the political year for ardent Democrats, but the racist stance taken by both of these patriarchs has dimmed their glorified position somewhat in more recent years. More recent Democratic presidents, and the Democratic Party, have favored a "non-literal" interpretation of the Constitution, which is to say, the context of the times allows the Supreme Court to issue decisions that violate strict construction of the Constitution. This allows the Democrats to avoid updating the Constitution via the amendment process, in which liberal views are heavily outnumbered and obtaining a vote of three-fourths of the states for a liberalization of the Constitution would be nearly impossible.

The first "Democrat," Thomas Jefferson, did not participate in the Constitutional Convention and later actively undermined it through authorship, with James Madison, of the Virginia and Kentucky Resolutions of 1798-1799 that attempted to make a case for the states being the final authority on constitutional issues. While he thought the Louisiana Purchase was unconstitutional, he proceeded with it anyway. Jefferson feared that a national government would turn monarchist, and he saw Alexander Hamilton, the most staunch of Federalists, as a man with monarchial ambitions. This fear no doubt played a large part in his antifederalist states-rights tendencies. The ironic death of Hamilton at the hands of Jefferson's arch-enemy, Aaron Burr (a fellow Antifederalist, sort of), did not lessen Jefferson's fears, and he continued his political machinations to prevent any elitists from taking power in the United States government. Jefferson unrealistically expected the United States to become a nation of yeoman farmers. He wanted no urban proletariat, who would be industrial workers, who he considered despicables. He thought that the nearly unlimited land to the west would allow all people without capital to eventually become self-sufficient small landowners. Unfortunately, most of the land included in the Louisiana Purchase, west of the Mississippi River into the Rocky Mountains, was and is unsuited to small-scale agriculture. For years part of it was identified as "The Great American Desert", later the "Dust Bowl". The victory for the small farmers, the Homestead Act, passed not by the Democrats who opposed it for pro-slavery reasons prior to the Civil War, when they controlled Congress, but by the Republicans, who have always been the party of entrepreneurship, large and small scale, worked in limited areas where small-scale farming was practical, but on the whole was a failure. Jefferson's true claim to fame, other than the Louisiana Purchase, came prior to his presidency when he was a member of Congress under the Articles of Confederation, when he prepared a preliminary Northwest Ordinance in 1784, although it was not adopted. Part of this was included in the Northwest Ordinance of 1787, which was truly a blueprint for the success of the middle class, particularly those small farmers, as the Northwest Ordinance allowed people of modest means to purchase small farms, and also banned slavery from the future states of Ohio, Indiana, Illinois, Michigan, and Wisconsin.

The second "Democrat," James Madison, while a key participant in the Constitutional Convention and a signer of the document, later came to agree with Jefferson that the federal government had too much power. James Monroe, the third president of this group, oversaw a divided government that was descending into chaos, as states-rights versus federal authority arguments moved to center stage.

The fourth, now officially "Democrat" president, Andrew Jackson, took personal authority over all issues, but destroyed the fiscal authority of the federal government by destroying the Second Bank of the United States. Jackson emasculated the Supreme Court by his refusal to enforce their decision in the question of Georgia versus the Cherokee Nation. He further destroyed the integrity of the Supreme Court by appointing a political hack, Roger B. Taney, as Chief Justice. Jackson's Specie Circular eliminated money from the economy, as banknotes became worthless (in truth, most were anyway) and people hoarded what gold and silver coin they had in their possession. Jackson's policies led directly to the worst depression felt by the people of the United States, a catastrophe that came about under his successor and political heir, Martin Van Buren. Survival of the nation under these conditions was in great part due to the higher percentage of the population that was living under survivalist conditions and was able to hunker down for the duration. Barter largely replaced money in the economic system, a condition that would have been intolerable in the 20th Century.

James K. Polk, the sixth Democrat President, was primarily concerned with preserving the ascendency of the slave power, by annexing the southwestern territory, which he assumed would join the Union as slave states. He was incorrect in this, as all the territory won in the Mexican War became free states, albeit all except California and Nevada did not enter the Union until after the end of the Civil War. "Arrizona" was briefly slave territory while the Confederates occupied it for a short time during the Civil War, but it was soon restored to New Mexico Territory.

The next two Democrat presidents, Franklin Pierce and James Buchanan, are universally considered the worst, or two of the worst, presidents the United States ever had, Pierce by approving the Kansas-Nebraska Act that led directly to the Civil War, and Buchanan by committing what many historians and political scientists consider treason by helping to arm the seceding southern states prior to the outbreak of the Civil War.

Andrew Johnson, a Democrat elected vice president under Abraham Lincoln, the Republican presidential candidate, became president upon Lincoln's assassination. Although none of this was Andrew Johnson's fault, he was never forgiven for any of it and was probably the most universally hated of any president. He mostly followed Lincoln's policies and intentions, particularly in regard to treatment of the postwar South, but was impeached, partly because of his lenient treatment of the former Confederacy, but mostly because he was a Democrat, and came as close as any president to being tried in the Senate and removed from office. He was selected as the vice presidential candidate by the Republicans, in desperation calling themselves the "Union" party, because war weariness made it seem certain that the Republicans could not win the 1864 election. As it turned out, Lincoln won rather handily with 55% of the vote, further alienating Johnson from the Republicans in power.

There were no further Democrat presidents until populism became a prevalent political movement. Grover Cleveland, while not a populist per se, ran for president as a Democrat, accepting Populist, Greenbacker, and anarchist votes in 1884, 1888, and 1892. He won the popular vote each time, but lost in the Electoral College to Benjamin Harrison in 1888. His presidency was largely ineffectual, as Congress was at least partially in the hands of the Republicans during his tenure in the White House and his conservative stance on some issues alienated some Democrat congressmen.

Woodrow Wilson, the next Democrat president, won office solely due to a personal feud between Theodore Roosevelt and William Howard Taft. Roosevelt, somewhat of a spoiled child and bully, was rejected by the Republican Party as their 1912 presidential candidate, in favor of Taft, who was just as much of a progressive as Roosevelt but seemed to be more amenable to conservative arguments. Roosevelt chose to run as a progressive third party candidate thus splitting the Republican vote, giving the election to Wilson, who only obtained 45% of the popular vote while winning 435 electoral votes (82%) to Roosevelt's 88 and 8 for Taft. Wilson was a hero of the American Left for decades, until it became clear that his Progressivism was for whites only. Wilson's chimerical approach to World War I and the peace that followed is the stuff of legend, while his dictatorial domestic policy was only equaled by the Alien and Sedition Acts of a century earlier. His nationalization of the railroads of the United States nearly destroyed them; ostensibly a war measure, it was in reality payback for railroad labor support. Permission for the president to take over the railroads was included in the Adamson Act, a measure signed by Wilson that avoided a railroad strike by granting most of the demands made by the railroad labor brotherhoods. Wilson was totally incapacitated after suffering a stroke while trying to campaign for support for his WWI peace treaty. He and his staff kept this a secret, so that his wife was, in effect, acting president for the last several months of his second term. The Democratic Party's crushing defeat in the 1920 election represented the public's opinion of Wilson's actions while president.

The tables were completely turned in 1932, when Franklin Delano Roosevelt was elected the next Democrat president. Herbert Hoover received all the blame for the depression that started in 1929, in spite of his initiation of several recovery measures that were eventually retained and expanded by Roosevelt, who received all the credit for them. Unfortunately, none of these measures really worked, and the economy of the United States did not really recover until World War II, when foreign demand for American goods, and American military spending, caused the economy to boom. Some economists and historians actually blame Roosevelt's more advanced New Deal measures for prolonging the depression by restraining recovery of the private sector. Keynesian economic theory, that governments can control the economy by controlling the money supply, was eventually proven correct, but the tremendous amount of deficit spending that it took to end the depression was only justified by the necessity of fighting World War II.

It can be justifiably said that Franklin Delano Roosevelt not only failed to end the depression, as the stopping of Hitler did that, but he also failed to win World War II. That war was started to prevent conquest of Poland by a totalitarian regime. In the aftermath of the war, not only Poland, but Estonia, Latvia, Lithuania, Czechoslovakia, Hungary, Romania, and Bulgaria (and a part of Germany) were firmly in the grip of the Union of Soviet Socialist Republics, a dictatorship under Joseph Stalin that was every bit as evil as Adolph Hitler's Germany.

Harry S. Truman was probably the most poorly prepared for his job of any president. This is another black mark against Franklin Delano Roosevelt, who should have been aware of his own fragile hold on life, and either given Truman some preparation for the job he was going to inherit, or picked a better-qualified vice president. Truman not only inherited Roosevelt's job, but also was saddled with Roosevelt's advisors and members of the executive department, many of whom were enamored of Joseph Stalin or who shared Roosevelt's foolish belief that Stalin could be handled. Directly, Truman was personally responsible for the outcome of the Potsdam Conference, which officially gave Stalin authority over most of Eastern Europe. Stalin took advantage of this to provide military assistance to allow the communists to take over the governments of many eastern European countries including Poland, Romania, Bulgaria, Hungary, Czechoslovakia, and eventually East Germany.

Second to Truman in being poorly prepared for his job was John F. Kennedy, who very narrowly won the presidency over Richard M. Nixon, the Republican candidate, in the 1960 election. It is possible that Kennedy's election was fraudulent, as there are rumors of illicit activity in the West Virginia Democrat primary of 1960, where Kennedy effectually knocked Hubert Humphrey out of the race for the Democratic Party's presidential nomination; and then later in the general election when Mayor Richard J. Daley found extra votes who-knows-where to give Kennedy Illinois' electoral votes and the election. Kennedy proceeded to stumble into one disaster after another, including the Bay of Pigs, Viet Nam, Berlin, and the Cuban Missile Crisis. In each of these, Kennedy's handlers were able to keep his image polished, with the help of the liberal press, while United States prestige withered around the world.

Lyndon Johnson took up where Kennedy left off, particularly in Viet Nam, which he turned into a colossal quagmire. Johnson was a very crafty politician, who saw that increasing wealth of the American middle class would likely turn the Republican Party into the majority party in United States politics. Johnson decided to counter that by "buying" the votes of minorities, particularly blacks, with his "Great Society" program that provided unprecedented entitlement and other benefits to minorities. Unfortunately, while the votes were gained for the Democrats, little improvement was gained in the lives of minority citizens, and the "race problem" got worse instead of better.

Jimmy Carter, the next Democrat president, was unable to acclimate himself to the Washington establishment, and accomplished little during his single term. He was one of the few elected presidents to lose his reelection contest. Carter somewhat anticipated the current left-wing political agenda with his policy of government as employer of last resort. It took years for the United States Postal Service to gradually come back to some semblance of reality after enduring Carter's "hire anyone and everyone" policy. Carter's policy of printing money to overcome government deficit spending resulted in unsustainable inflation, wreaking havoc in American industry and leading to the "Rust Belt."

William Jefferson Clinton was the first Democrat to declare he was running for president in 1992. Most leading potential candidates for the Democrat nomination had concluded in 1991 that George Herbert Walker Bush was unbeatable, and decided to sit out the 1992 election. After Bush suffered a dramatic, steep drop in popularity, Clinton was an easy victor in the 1992 general election in spite of his apparent lightweight status and his less than stellar run as Governor of Arkansas. Clinton made an attempt at resuming and going beyond Carter's policies, but after a stinging defeat for the Democrats in the midterm elections of 1994 he switched from liberal to conservative, or at least neutral, in his proposed policies. After gutting the military and using the peace dividend to balance the budget, he easily won reelection in 1996. In spite of scandal after scandal, he maintained his popularity, with the help of the liberal media, and survived impeachment.

Barrack Obama, another Democrat politician with little in his background to suggest he was qualified for the presidency, won the 2008 presidential election handily. He proceeded to push a liberal domestic policy and what could only be called an anti-American foreign policy, lost the House of Representatives to the Republicans in 2010, and saw Congress go Republican in both House and Senate in 2014. He won reelection in 2012 mostly because of an indifferent conservative turnout for the Republican presidential nominee, Mitt Romney, similar to what happened in the 2008 presidential election with John McCain as the Republican nominee.

CHAPTER 3 – THE REPUBLICAN PRESIDENTS

The Republicans could be called the Conservative Party, not unlike their counterparts in Canada and Great Britain, with whom they are often in alliance on issues common to their respective countries, such as in the rapport between Ronald Reagan and Margaret Thatcher. Heirs, via the Whigs, to the Federalist mantle, the Republicans have generally maintained a strict-constructionist view of the United States Constitution. In spite of being more in tune with the letter of the Constitution, there have been more strong Republican presidents than strong Democrat presidents, but only by a margin of eight to seven. There have, however, been more weak Republican presidents than weak Democrats, by a slightly larger margin of nine to six. Moderates are again more nearly equal, eight Republicans to seven Democrats (see Appendix D2 for a more detailed picture of strong vs weak presidents). The Republicans can claim the only completely unelected president, Gerald Ford, helping to give them more weak presidents.

George Washington acted the disinterested patriotic statesman throughout his career, although his investment in western lands benefitted greatly via the independence of the United States. Although not a member of a political party, as such did not officially exist when Washington became president, Washington consistently favored the policies of his Secretary of the Treasury, Alexander Hamilton, over those of Thomas Jefferson, Secretary of State. Some historians claim that Washington was unduly influenced by Hamilton, and Washington's prestige did, in fact, decline late in his presidency as party politics took center stage with Jefferson's withdrawal from the cabinet to become the leader of the "Republican" Party, composed primarily of former Antifederalists. Washington generally followed strict constitutional guidelines in his presidency, although he did establish many precedents that continued in force long after his retirement.

John Adams was the first, and last, official Federalist president. He believed the president was the chief statesman and Chief of State, and expected to be treated accordingly. He ran into difficulties with his Federalist colleagues, who saw Alexander Hamilton as the true leader of the party, and more or less ignored Adams.

In spite of this, Adams continued the work of Washington in establishing the mechanics of United States government, including providing for a permanent Navy. Adams also improved the international prestige of the United States by his handling of the XYZ affair, successfully resisting French attempts to interfere in the United States government.

John Quincy Adams can be considered the next Federalist, or Whig, or Republican president, although the only national political party at the time was the "Republican" party of Thomas Jefferson, which was in the process of splitting into the short-lived National Republicans and Democratic Republicans. John Quincy Adams is generally regarded as the only National Republican president. Henry Clay, leader of the National Republicans, ran against Andrew Jackson in 1832 in lieu of John Quincy Adams, and lost.

William Henry Harrison, the next Republican (of the modern variety) president, elected as a Whig, spent his entire presidency in sickbed, and died before performing any presidential duties other than reading his inauguration speech. He was replaced by his vice president, John Tyler, a former Democrat, who joined the Whigs in protest of Andrew Jackson's imperial policies, and reverted to the Democratic Party agenda after becoming president.

Zachary Taylor, the sixth Republican president, was also elected as a Whig, and like William Henry Harrison was a war hero, which probably helped him to get elected. Unfortunately, also like William Henry Harrison, Taylor died in office. He served long enough to make an effort to solve some of the insoluble problems facing the country at the time, but his political naivete was apparent to all and his proposals, although quite sensible, were not taken seriously by the professional politicians in Washington.

Millard Fillmore, Taylor's vice president, took over for the remainder of Taylor's term, but accomplished little as he was faced with a hostile Democratic Congress throughout his tenure as president.

The next Republican president, Abraham Lincoln, a former Whig who joined the Republican Party after its creation, is almost universally ranked as the best, or the second-best, of all presidents. In the face of intense opposition, Lincoln solved the slavery dilemma that had severely troubled the nation since the Constitutional Convention. Some authorities blame Lincoln for starting the Civil War, but the slave states' use of secession as the solution to the slavery crisis was clearly unacceptable, and all other efforts of remediation had failed. Lincoln's stated purpose on running for, being elected, and taking office as president was to preserve the Union. Lincoln initially denied any intent to free the slaves of the South, but often expressed his opposition to slavery, and his belief that it would eventually dwindle to nothingness. Lincoln was strongly opposed to dissolution of the Union, perhaps recognizing the predicament that western farmers would be in if their crops would have to be exported through a foreign country should Arkansas and Louisiana, as well as Tennessee and Mississippi, through which the Mississippi River flows on its way to the Gulf of Mexico, be allowed to leave the United States with the rest of the Confederacy. Lincoln eventually decided that emancipation of the slaves was a necessity, but was assassinated before he could help push through the 13th Amendment abolishing slavery. This task was left to his vice president, Andrew Johnson, who, although a Democrat, assumed the presidency upon Lincoln's death.

Ulysses S. Grant, the first of a series of post-Civil-War Republican presidents, presided over most of the Reconstruction Era. He largely deferred to Congress on most issues, but his prestige as the victor in the Civil War allowed him great influence on the issues of the day.

Rutherford B. Hayes, the tenth Republican president, was the first to be elected with a majority of the electoral vote but with a minority of the popular vote. Hayes won the electoral vote as the result of a compromise that decided the winner of several disputed electoral votes. Samuel Tilden, the Democratic Party contender, clearly won a majority of the popular vote, and possibly would have won the electoral vote if the distribution of the disputed electoral votes had been completely unbiased. Not unlike John Quincy Adams previously, under similar circumstances but perhaps more justifiably, Hayes was hounded throughout his presidency with cries of fraud and served a somewhat unhappy single term.

Not unlike William Henry Harrison, James A. Garfield, the next Republican president, was not in office long enough to make his mark. Shot by a deranged, disappointed office-seeker only four months after taking office, Garfield lingered for a little over two months before dying.

Chester Alan Arthur was Garfield's vice president, a compromise candidate from the Stalwart section of the party, whom no one expected to ever become president. Assumed to be a corrupt spoils man, Arthur surprised everyone by his virtuous presidency, which included the first meaningful steps toward a nonpartisan civil service.

Benjamin Harrison was the grandson of William Henry Harrison, and little more was expected of him than his grandfather accomplished in office. Benjamin Harrison considered it the duty of his office to administer laws passed by Congress; he had neither the desire nor the ability to provide leadership to the legislative branch, which was only briefly controlled by the Republicans during his term anyway. His loss of the popular vote in the election of 1888 did not provide him with any mandate.

William McKinley, the fourteenth Federalist/Whig/Republican president, was considered somewhat spineless by many, including even a few of his closest colleagues. He was fortunate enough to preside over an era of unprecedented increase in prosperity, shared by almost the entire population of the United States, from carriers of the "full dinner pail" to the wealthiest of the "robber barons". This prosperity was in fact largely the result of the economic and governmental policies promulgated by McKinley and his Republican cohorts. The Republican Party remained in control in Washington, except for a very brief period, until 1931.

Theodore Roosevelt became the youngest President of the United States ever when William McKinley was assassinated in September 1901. Roosevelt was hardly welcomed with open arms by the business community, as he was an ardent progressive, and soon began "trust-busting," expanding national parks and forests, and performing other acts that truly frightened the economic power groups of the country.

William Howard Taft was elected the sixteenth Republican president in 1908. He continued Roosevelt's progressive policies, and even expanded upon them. He was a rather colorless chief executive, however, and did not excite the approbation of the masses. Roosevelt had hand-picked Taft as his successor, but after four years decided that Taft was not the man to be trusted to continue Roosevelt's progressive program. Roosevelt challenged Taft for the

1912 Republican nomination for president, but the party leaders decided Roosevelt was too radical, and selected Taft as the party's nominee. Roosevelt immediately turned to the progressives, pushed aside their leader, Robert M. La Follette, and became the progressive, or "Bull Moose" party's nominee for president in 1912. This practically guaranteed the election of the Democratic Party's nominee (Woodrow Wilson) by splitting the Republican vote.

Woodrow Wilson, by maneuvering the United States into World War I on the side of the Allies, guaranteed their victory over Germany. He did not realize, or perhaps ignored, the many secret pacts and treaties the Allies had among themselves, that never could have been enforced except with the help of the United States in bringing Germany to the peace table, hat in hand. The resulting peace practically guaranteed a continuation of the war as soon as Germany could build up enough strength to resume it. While the people of the United States might not have seen World War II coming, they did see that Wilson was trying, with his Fourteen Points that were a critical part of the Versailles Treaty ending World War I, to force the United States into a leading position as policeman to keep the future peace. They resoundingly rejected this role by giving Warren Gamaliel Harding and the Republicans an over-whelming landslide victory in the 1920 presidential election. Harding received 63.8% of the popular vote, the highest percentage ever recorded. While Harding made some significant positive accomplishments during his short presidency of only 2-1/2 years, he is remembered today almost exclusively for the malfeasance in office of several of his cabinet members.

Calvin Coolidge became the 18th Republican president on the death of Warren Harding but was elected on his own in 1924. Coolidge was extremely popular, particularly among the middle class, as increased industrial and agricultural production provided prosperity for all, except for American farmers, as increased production combined with reduced worldwide demand meant lower prices for them. Coolidge perhaps saw trouble ahead as the rest of the world slowly got into competition with the United States for the production and supply of goods and services. He chose not to run again for president in 1928.

Herbert Hoover received the Republican nomination for president in 1928 and was an easy victor in the general election. His joy was short lived, as the stock market crashed less than a year into his presidency, followed by recession, and then outright depression. Hoover could not avoid taking the fall for the depression, in spite of his innovative efforts to mitigate its effects. He received little assistance in his efforts from a hostile Congress, and was overwhelmingly defeated in his reelection bid in 1932.

Dwight Eisenhower was solicited by both the Democrats and Republicans as their presidential candidate in 1952. As the great hero of World War II, he was universally admired and believed to be a competent leader. Eisenhower said yes to the Republicans, perhaps because he felt Franklin Roosevelt and Harry Truman were too easily manipulated by Joseph Stalin. Eisenhower went on to easy victories in the 1952 and 1956 presidential elections although the Democrats took over control of both houses of Congress. It would appear that his "I like Ike" popularity was more personal than ideological.

Richard Nixon was Dwight Eisenhower's vice president from 1953 to 1961. He appeared to be a bit more conservative than Eisenhower, and was an ardent anti-Communist. He was eventually proved correct in his allegations that Alger Hiss, a Democratic Party hero, was a communist, but was never forgiven by liberals for pushing the issue. He had personality issues that became overwhelmingly prominent later in his presidency, but he successfully overcame them during the 1968 presidential campaign during which he appeared publicly as a carefree, good-humored man about town. He barely defeated Hubert Humphrey in the 1968 election, due largely to the 3rd party candidacy of George Wallace, which took the votes of many of the more conservative citizens.

The resignation of Richard Nixon after the Watergate scandal gave the presidency to Gerald Ford, who was appointed to the office of vice president after the resignation in disgrace of Spiro Agnew, who was elected with Richard Nixon in 1972. Ford thus became the only completely non-elected President of the United States. Ford was initially quite popular, but his pardoning of Richard Nixon and the sliding of the country into an economic recession, combined with several gaffes of large and small moment brought his popularity to an end and he was one of the few sitting presidents to lose his reelection bid.

In spite of, or perhaps because of, being governor of California, ex-actor Ronald Reagan was not taken seriously as a presidential candidate in 1976 or early in the 1980 campaign. But he surprised everyone in 1980 with a massive defeat of the incumbent, Jimmy Carter. Reagan went on to achieve immense popularity as president and in his reelection campaign of 1984 came as close as anyone since James Monroe in 1820 to winning 100% of the electoral vote, only losing one state (Minnesota) and the District of Columbia.

George Herbert Walker Bush, after being severely critical of Ronald Reagan during the primary campaign in 1980, went on to be his running mate on the Republican ticket in both 1980 and 1984. Bush had an extremely high approval rating as he began his presidency but was one of the most unpopular presidents ever by the time of the 1992 election. He lost the support of conservatives by raising taxes after he said he wouldn't (actually he said, "No new taxes"), and he antagonized liberals with a less than heartfelt approach to poor relief. He also came off as weak in several critical situations, and the "wimp factor" became an issue.

George Walker Bush, the son of George Herbert Walker Bush, became the 25th Republican president while winning fewer popular votes than his opponent, Al Gore, in the 2000 presidential election. Florida's defective ballots in the presidential election forced the decision on who won Florida's 2000 electoral vote to the United States Supreme Court. The Court, with seven Republican-appointed justices and only 2 Democrat-appointed judges, declared Bush the winner. Democrats cried foul, but there was no possible appeal.

Donald Trump was one more Republican presidential candidate to win the Electoral College while his Democrat opponent, Hillary Rodham Clinton in this case, received more popular votes than the winner. Clinton did not receive a majority of the popular vote (she got 48.90%), but this did not prevent her and the Democratic Party from crying foul, and continuing to cry foul throughout Trump's (presumptive) first term, to the point of beginning, in October 2019, impeachment proceedings in the House of Representatives. Up to this point (April 2020), Trump has successfully deflected each Democratic Party assault on his presidency, but these activities have gone on continuously since before Trump was inaugurated. The Democrat-controlled House of Representatives voted to impeach the president, and brought charges in the Senate, but Trump was acquitted on all counts. In the meantime, Trump has effectively used Executive Orders and what few laws that have been passed to accomplish much of his pronounced agenda, and the country has been on a continuous prosperity ride that appeared likely to continue to the 2020 election, but for a viral pandemic that arrived in late Winter.

CHAPTER 4 – RANKING THE PRESIDENTS

In many countries, the government's chief executive is chosen by the legislature in a parliamentary type of government. As long as that chief executive has a party that controls the legislature, he or she usually remains in office. In the United States, the chief executive, the President, is chosen wholly independently from the legislature, and as is discussed above frequently is at odds with the legislature, which may be controlled by a political party other than that of the President. The means of choosing the President of the United States is somewhat convoluted, very indirect, and not particularly democratic. Electors from each state gather to cast their votes for President in the Electoral College, and these votes are counted by the President of the Senate. The winner of a majority of the votes that are cast wins. Each state gets two electoral votes plus one elector for each member it has in the House of Representatives. There are an additional three votes for the District of Columbia. The total number of electors is set by law at 538 so that to win the presidency, a candidate has to collect at least 270 votes in the electoral college. It is important to realize that each elector can vote for whomever they wish; there is no federal law mandating that they vote for the winner of any election, although some states require their electors to do so. It is therefore quite true that anyone can grow up to become President of the United States, provided they meet the Constitutional requirements to qualify. In practice, the Electors are strongly pressured by convention to vote for the winner of a state's popular vote for president. In most states it is winner take all, but a few smaller states require their electors to be split to reflect the popular vote. There was a movement at one time for a constitutional amendment to have the electors of each state proportioned based on the popular vote, but this effort failed (see page 108). A review of this process by the Supreme Court may be upcoming. A look at close elections suggests that such a change would not affect the outcome, but would make the electoral vote closer.

The Constitution is very clear on the duties of the President. Per Article II, ''Before he enter on the execution of his Office, he shall take the following Oath or Affirmation: "I do solemnly swear (or affirm) that I will faithfully execute the office of President of the United States, and will to the best of my Ability preserve, protect and defend the Constitution of the United States". The Constitution also requires that the President is Commander in Chief of the armed forces of the United States, and the militia when called into federal service. The President may require the opinion in writing of any of the principal officers of the government of United States, and may grant reprieves and pardons, but not in cases of impeachment. The President may make treaties with sovereign nations, but must have the concurrence of two thirds of the Senate. The President with the concurrence of the Senate appoints ambassadors, Supreme Court justices, and other officers of the United States. The President is required to inform Congress of the State of the Union on a regular basis. The President receives ambassadors and other public ministers. The President is to "take care that the laws be faithfully executed." The President commissions all officers (military) of the United States. The above constitutes the entire Constitutional duties of the President. No amendment to the Constitution to date has altered these duties.

Rating the President on how he or she performs his (or her, assuming the Constitution allows a woman to be President (see excerpt in above paragraph)) Constitutional duties is very difficult, as the details of the above duties are rather complicated and can be open to interpretation. There is also the question of implied powers. And finally, the laws as passed by Congress can in some cases be somewhat ambiguous and contradictory. This book rates the presidents of the United States based on four (4) factors (see Appendix A): 1) Did they help make America great? 2) Did the quality of life of the American People improve under their presidency? 3) Did they rise to the occasion when a crisis arose? 4) How much opposition did they have in doing their jobs? Other minor factors or special cases arose, which modified the rating in some cases. In order to quantitatively rank the presidents, each of the four primary factors is given a weight, and each president is given a rating of zero to ten on how he fared in each category. There are objective criteria, such as real growth in Gross National Product, increase in national wealth, increase in population, increase in size of territory, which could be used to rate presidents, but as all these could be the result of factors beyond a president's control, or even contrary to a president's intentions, they are not explicitly used here. Subjective evaluations are used almost exclusively in preparing these ratings. Some accomplishments are attributed to a particular president to a greater or lesser degree, even though he may have had little or no influence on them. Some accomplishments were the results of a particularly effective Secretary of State, or events outside the control of the government in Washington, but are here given as credit to the president at the time, unless he was actively working against such accomplishments. Efforts to accomplish certain goals are included, even though the goal in question may not have been reached.

The weights:

1)	Making America Great	10
2)	Improving Quality of Life	8
3)	Meeting Crises	10
4)	Overcoming Opposition	8

The total potential maximum score is thus 36.0. There is no "curve" or other weighing mechanism, and the scores are not comparative, so that it is potentially possible that every president could get a perfect score of 36.0, or any or all presidents could be above or below the 50% score of 18.0. A score of 18.0 is considered neutral, although a president may achieve an overall score of 18 while having higher scores in one or more categories while having lower scores in other categories. As it happens, in the Real Ranking twenty presidents received an above average score of more than 18.0 and twenty presidents received an overall score of less than 18.0. Of the four presidents (excluding Trump) who received an average score of 18.0, three received scores of 50% in all categories.

Popularity is not a factor in the Real Ranking ratings; personality does not enter into the mix except as it may weigh into a president's ability to lead others into his point of view. The majority of modern historians appear to be more interested in star power than in effectiveness when ranking the presidents and the more common rankings that have been published and have appeared on television or other media appear to reflect this. They do not, as a rule, refer to this quality as popularity, but use the phrase, "ability to inspire", or something similar, and consistently give it high influence in their rankings. The mainstream rankings also tend to favor "Robin Hood" types, who, simplistically speaking, favor taxing the rich to support the poor. Considering that it is estimated that 78% of Americans live paycheck to paycheck*, although not all, by any means, are in poverty, popularity and the Robin Hood image can be synonymous. Of nine Robin Hood presidents (Jefferson, Jackson, Theodore Roosevelt, Wilson, Franklin Delano Roosevelt, Truman, Lyndon Johnson, Clinton, and Obama), all are in the top 18 of the composite or aggregate mainstream poll, while all are in the bottom 25 of the libertarian ranking. All, notably, are Democrats except for Theodore Roosevelt, who some say was a closet Democrat. The Real Ranking has two in the top ten (Jefferson and Theodore Roosevelt) and the others in the bottom eleven. The Robin Hood syndrome reached a peak with the liberal concept of the post-industrial state, where the middle class would be taxed to support all those who lost means of self-support as manufacturing jobs left the United States for Mexico and Asia. Unfortunately for the liberals, most blue-collar types prefer jobs to welfare, resulting in such phenomena as the "Reagan Revolution," the Republican "Contract with America," and the Trump victory in 2016.

A third factor, and perhaps the most important, in ranking, which seems to be a major one for historians, is willingness to usurp constitutional powers. The most activist presidents are consistently at the top of the mainstream presidential rankings, and also at the top of the popularity rankings, as the president is generally considered to be the representative of the people in Washington while Congress is generally considered to be the tool of special interests and lobbyists. The ten most active presidents, Theodore Roosevelt, Wilson, Lincoln, Franklin Delano Roosevelt, Kennedy, Lyndon Johnson, Jefferson, Jackson, Polk, and Truman are all, except for Polk, at the top of most presidential popularity polls. The ten least active presidents, William Henry Harrison, Benjamin Harrison, Garfield, Buchanan, Fillmore, Coolidge, Harding, Arthur,

---

*per CareerBuilder.com (2017), cited by CBS News and Forbes Magazine.

Grant, and Andrew Johnson, are consistently at the bottom of the popularity polls. This is confirmed in a way, as the libertarians, who are usually the most adamant strict-constructionists regarding the Constitution, consistently favor the least-popular presidents.

Several mainstream presidential rankings were tabulated by Wikipedia (see Chapter 14, page 143). The different mainstream rankings tend to agree on ranking the more popular presidents, but differ more widely with unpopular presidents. The ranking spreads for the more popular presidents, such as Washington, Jefferson, Lincoln, and Franklin Delano Roosevelt were 3, 5, 2, and 2, respectively (William Henry Harrison and James A. Garfield are excluded as many felt their terms were too short to be evaluated, and Grover Cleveland's two non-consecutive terms were combined for rating purposes). For Andrew Johnson the spread in ranking was 24 when measuring from best to worst, the largest range of any president (his range when measuring worst to best was only 11). Herbert Hoover and Martin Van Buren, two very unpopular presidents who had the misfortune to serve during the onset of depressions, both had ranking spreads of 19 (best to worst). When measuring worst to best, their spreads were 14 and 12, respectively (See Appendix D and Appendix F).

The most popular presidents were in the top ten in terms of composite rankings from the nineteen sources cited by Wikipedia: Lincoln, Franklin Delano Roosevelt, Washington, Theodore Roosevelt, Jefferson, Truman, Wilson, Eisenhower, Jackson, and Kennedy. The Real Ranking as shown in Chapters 5, 6, and 7 ("great" down to "better-than-average") only includes five of these in their top ten: Washington, Lincoln, Jefferson, Theodore Roosevelt, and Eisenhower. In a more radical stance, the libertarian Ivan Eland, in his book *Recarving Rushmore*, (2014)*, rates 42 presidents on "peace, prosperity, and liberty." He ranks Grover Cleveland once, combining his two non-consecutive terms into one rating, much like most other rankings. Eland does not evaluate the brief presidencies of William Henry Harrison and James A. Garfield, nor does he evaluate Donald Trump, who had not yet been elected in 2014. His ranking of "presidential success" has in his top ten only Washington and Eisenhower of the popular presidents listed above.

Recarving Rushmore: Ranking the Presidents on Peace, Prosperity, and Liberty (Oakland: Independent Institute 2014)

Eland's top four presidential successes are all among the least popular presidents. In order: John Tyler, Grover Cleveland, Martin Van Buren, and Rutherford B. Hayes. The libertarian philosophy zeroes in on strict constructionism as far as the Constitution is concerned. The president, in their point of view, is only there for his explicitly enumerated Constitutional responsibilities, overlooking the nebulous clause in Article II Section 3: "He shall...recommend to their (Congress') Consideration such Measures as he shall judge necessary and expedient," and must look to Congress for all initiatives. Eland's top four presidents achieved his top places by default: They were unpopular with the public and had no or little support in Congress, even among their own party, so were unable to accomplish much beyond at least a part of their bare minimum Constitutional duties.

The Real Ranking and Eland's libertarian ranking allow zero credit for generating enthusiasm among one's constituents. Eland sets much more restrictive goals for the president than does Real Ranking. On the other hand, historians and pundits seem to like to see a president who takes the initiative and pushes his agenda, particularly if it is popular with the public, and wins Congress to his side, or goes around Congress as long as he has strong support among the public. Some detailed comparisons between different rankings are in later chapters and in Appendix D, Appendix E, and Appendix F. The generally very low opinion most members of the public have for Congress (except for their own congressperson, who usually gets reelected), gives the president some leeway to go beyond the Constitution in pursuing his agenda as long his public opinion poll numbers are higher than those of Congress, which is usually the case.

The Constitution leaves to the states some of the details on electing presidents, although there are several clauses and a few amendments (see pages x-xii, 25, and 130) that provide some restrictions. Originally, the electors were chosen primarily by the state legislatures. New states that entered the union tended to be more democratic, choosing the electors by popular vote of a substantial percentage of the population. Eventually the older states were more or less forced by popular pressure to follow the same procedures, so that by the election of 1824 popular vote was a major factor in presidential elections.

The party identifications usually associated with presidents are modern-day Democrat or Republican. Almost all earlier major-party identifications led to one or the other of these. Therein lies a major source of confusion when discussing party politics in the United States. When political parties were first formed on a national level in the United States, the more conservative party chose the name "Federalist," in keeping with their nationalistic goals of increased power in the central government by means of the Constitution. People more concerned with maintaining state's rights and preventing the growth of an omnipotent central government that would likely favor large financial interests were "Antifederalists". After the Antifederalists were somewhat forced by events to accept the Constitution, the word "Antifederalist" was no longer appropriate, so they chose a new name, "Republican," in keeping with their enthusiasm for things French (after their Revolution, during the First Republic), where the word originated. They briefly became Democratic Republicans, then they dropped the word "Republican" during Andrew Jackson's presidency and became simply "Democrats." Unfortunately, the Whigs, the party of opposite intentions, formed mainly to obstruct Andrew Jackson, no longer had a valid name after the retirement of Jackson from politics, and did not represent many of the people who opposed the Democratic Party in the 1850s. When a new party was formed in 1854 in Ripon, Wisconsin (and Jackson, Michigan), combining most of the Whigs with the opponents of the extension of slavery who had partially organized as the Free-Soil Party, the perfectly good name of "Republican" was resurrected. Some presidents were associated with third parties before or after their presidencies but were identified with a major party while president.

Previous major parties and their modern equivalents are as follows:

Federalist	becomes	Republican (R)(1854-present)
Antifederalist	becomes	Democrat (D)
Republican (1792-1828)	becomes	Democrat (D)
		or Republican (R) in 1 case, John Quincy Adams
Democratic Republican	becomes	Democrat (D)
National Republican	becomes	Republican (R)
Whig	becomes	Republican (R)

The demise of the Federalist Party did not immediately result in the creation of a new party that represented the views of those persons who had called themselves Federalists. The Federalist Party remained in existence after 1800, until about 1828, although it did not put up a candidate for president after

1816. Eventually, in opposition to the regal presidency of Andrew Jackson, the Whig party was organized, modeled after the British Whig party that was primarily, at least originally, interested in opposing the power of the king.

For a period of approximately eight years, from about 1820 to 1828, there was only one major political party in the United States, the "Republicans", founded by Thomas Jefferson in the very late 18th Century to combat Alexander Hamilton's Federalists. Needless to say, this name, "Republican" would be a point of confusion regarding politics in the United States between 1788 and 1850 if it had not been largely ignored by most historians, who generally use the name "Democratic Republican" although it was not invented until the 1820s, when the "Republican" Party split into Democratic Republicans (to become Democrats) and National Republicans (to become Whigs). These earlier "Republicans" were former Antifederalists who decided to change their party's name after the Constitution was adopted. They are the party of Thomas Jefferson, and thus the predecessors of the Democratic Party, and definitely not associated with the modern Republican Party, which got its start in the 1850s, long after the early "Republicans" became Democrats. The majority of the early "Republicans" became, briefly, Democratic Republicans, and then, when Jackson was president, became officially Democrats. Some say that the second Republican Party did, however, take its name consciously from the first "Republican Party", in recognition of Thomas Jefferson's role in making the United States a great democracy.

Both major political parties in the United States changed not only their names but also their purpose as time went on. Originally, the Antifederalist-"Republicans" were the party of the self-sufficient small landowners, who saw no need for government oversight and had small amounts of cash available to pay taxes; this made them very resistant to big government. Now 200 years later the Democratic Party is very much the party of big government, promoting high taxes and high government expenditures at the national level and very little discretion at the state government level. The Federalists originally favored control of the economy at the national level with minimal discretion allowed by the state governments, and high federal taxes to pay for national public works such as canals and railroads, and a quasigovernmental national banking system. Today's Republican Party generally avoids national funding of public works projects although exceptions are made, and encourages greater flexibility and responsibility in most areas at the state government level.

Locofocos, Barnburners, Free Soilers and the 1850s American Party never elected a president, in spite of some persons who became president having been at one time before or after their presidency affiliated with one of these party labels. Nor did any of the later third parties such as Greenbackers and Populists, and, more modern-day third parties, Socialist, Green, Libertarian, et al, produce any presidents. Former president Millard Fillmore, running in 1856 under the American ("Know-Nothing") Party (secret, anti-immigrant, anti-Catholic) ticket, won 8 electoral votes and may have thrown the election to James Buchanan. Robert La Follete, a former Republican running for President as a Progressive in 1924, won the 12 electoral votes of his home state of Wisconsin and the Progressive Party continues in existence to this day. Strom Thurmond, in 1948, won 39 electoral votes as the "States Rights Democratic Party" candidate for president. This "party" ran no other candidates and its members mostly returned to their roots in the national Democratic Party after the 1948 election.

The Progressive Party mentioned above has had a resurgence in recent years as millennials and others have called for increased redistribution of wealth, to the point of resuscitating the "soak the rich" policies advocated by some prior to World War II. This is somewhat ironic as the Progressive Party originated as a movement within the Republican Party to protect the middle class, including small-business entrepreneur types, against the depredations of "robber barons" such as John D. Rockefeller. The progressive movement quickly became general, with both Republican and Democrat politicians in the early 20th century jumping on the bandwagon. When it became an independent party, in the election of 1912, it came in second in the popular vote nationwide. The progressive movement moved rather quickly to the left, and one of the originators of the movement, Robert M. La Follette, reconstituted the Progressive Party after World War I as a frankly socialistic organization, which it remains today.

To make matters clear, there have always been only two major political parties in the United States, and each has always primarily represented a certain group of people, although their stated political philosophies have changed over time, particularly that of what is now the Democratic Party. For a brief period, in the prosperous 1950s and early 1960s, there was little to differentiate between the two parties, but throughout most of United States history they have been bitterly opposed. This was particularly true from Andrew Jackson's time up to the Civil War. It has also been more true recently, as the two major parties have each developed conflicting philosophies.

The Federalists of the 18ᵗʰ Century stood for a stronger national government, particularly in financial matters, at the expense of the states. They then metamorphosed into the Whigs, which stood for strong central government influence on the economy, particularly by means of internal improvements, a national bank, and restrictive tariffs, but limitation of the central power, particularly the president, primarily a response to the many unconstitutional moves by Andrew Jackson, who sincerely (and correctly) felt that he had the mass of the people behind him in anything he chose to do. When the Whigs, along with the Free-Soil Party and the American Party, joined the Republican Party of 1856, they developed a stronger nationalist stance against the states-right southern Democrats, primarily to prevent the expansion of slavery into the territories and possibly into the free states. The modern Republicans reverted to a more states-rights stance in the 20ᵗʰ Century, opposing the extension of New Deal-type programs into areas that were felt to be the domain of the states per the Constitution.

The Antifederalists, as noted above, quickly changed their name to "Republicans", and were led by Thomas Jefferson as advocates of the farmers, the predominant economic group of the country. They were in natural opposition to the merchants and bankers who formed the core of the membership of the Federalist Party. These "Republicans" became essentially the only national political party in the United States after the War of 1812, and had only token Federalist Party opposition in the presidential election of 1816. The Federalists did not put up a presidential candidate in 1820 or 1824, leaving the field to the "Republicans". These "Republicans" split due to ideological differences into National Republicans and Democratic Republicans by 1828. The Democratic Republicans became simply Democrats, and most of the National Republicans became Whigs. The Democrats and their predecessors have consistently claimed to be the champions of the "common man," and originally were definitely the party of the typical citizen; but gradually moved to being advocate of the lowest class of society until today their primary constituency is all the people who look to the government to supply at least a portion of their basic needs, that is to say, the welfare advocate party. While Thomas Jefferson sincerely felt, at least in regard to the federal government, that "that governs best which governs the least" (see page 45), and the Democratic Party for many decades after Jefferson was the states-rights party, the modern Democratic Party strongly favors nationalism and severe limitations on the rights of states to go their own way.

The Federalists originally were supporters of a stronger national government as opposed to the loose confederation of states under the Articles of Confederation. Most people were perfectly happy living under limited government that was largely, in the various statehouses, firmly democratic with a small "d." These persons were not particularly concerned about the long-term effects of the weakness of the United States on the international scene. Merchants, bankers, and other capitalists suffered the most under the near anarchy situation that prevailed from 1776 to 1787. This group, along with the wealthier plantation owners such as George Washington, and middle class professional persons such as John Adams, were able to convince people, at the various state conventions, to support the Constitution in spite of grave misgivings on the part of many of their fellow citizens. Voting for delegates to the various state ratifying conventions was reported to be light, apparently due to lack of interest, even among those few who held the voting franchise at that time. Rhode Island, for instance, had a popular vote on ratification in March of 1788, when the Constitution lost, 237 to 2708. The population of Rhode Island at the time was about 68,000.

In the voting population of the United States as a whole, the Federalists were in a minority from the beginning, although this was a time when greater restrictions on suffrage kept most people from voting, even many adult white males. As more and more states opened the franchise to all or most adult white males in the early 19th Century, the Federalist became more and more a minority party until they disappeared completely. The Federalist reincarnation as Whigs and then Republicans did not erase their minority status, except briefly when slavery became the overwhelming topic of political discussion in the 1850s, and the Democratic Party became synonymous with treason in the 1860s. Although Republicans dominated the presidency from the Civil War until the Great Depression, the Democratic Party often controlled at least one house of Congress in this period. The popular vote in presidential elections of this period was usually quite close; twice between 1868 and 1900 the Republican candidate won the election while gaining fewer popular votes than his Democrat opponent.

The Democratic Party has been, throughout United States history, the democratic party, usually favoring wider suffrage, although Thomas Jefferson, the first Democrat, had no use for the urban proletariat. He was a staunch advocate for the yeoman farmer, an independent tiller of the soil. This was largely behind the anti-slavery and pro-small landowner clauses in his proposed Northwest Ordinance of 1784. Andrew Jackson, the first president elected officially as a Democrat, was more a hater of the privileged classes, particularly bankers, than he was a favorer of the lower classes, but he was embraced wholeheartedly by the poorest sector of the population, and tied them more-or-less permanently to the Democratic Party.

CHAPTER 5 – THE GREAT PRESIDENTS

Very few presidents have attained greatness. The opportunity to seize an historic moment and make the most of it does not come to everyone. George Washington had a clean slate to make the Presidency, and the nation, what he thought they should be. Abraham Lincoln faced destruction of the Union, and found the means to save it. Ronald Reagan saw an opportunity to end a destructive world situation and took it.

1)   George Washington, No Party but in Sympathy with the Federalists
George Washington is correctly identified as the father of his country, but he can also be called the father of the United States government. After presiding at the constitutional convention of 1787, he then filled the first two presidential terms from 1789 to 1797. While president, he personally established many of the unwritten protocols of government operation and successfully wielded his extensive powers to secure the existence of the new government in spite of its lackluster support among the general population. Most importantly, he resisted the temptation to grasp absolute power, which would have in all likelihood been granted to him for life if he wished it, and instead retired voluntarily after two terms in office. Washington disdained political parties but sympathized with the Federalists. The first Congress, inaugurated in 1789, was in sympathy with Washington, but party differences soon broke out and Washington was faced with strong Antifederalist or "Republican" (call it Democratic Republican) opposition for the remainder of his time in office.

Washington was a real estate speculator and was highly interested in the lands beyond the Appalachian Mountains. He was one of the first to propose improved communications between the settled east and the developing west. With his knowledge of surveying, a substantial part of the 18th Century civil engineering curriculum, he is credited with being an original proposer of the Chesapeake and Ohio Canal, intended to link tidewater on the Potomac River in what was to become Washington, D.C., with the Ohio River.

Regarding the qualities by which the presidents are evaluated, Washington fares as follows:

1) Making America Great

    There is hardly any question that the United States today would not exist if it were not for George Washington's courageous leadership in forming and holding together the country after the contentious adoption of the Constitution. Washington organized the new government, with Hamilton's help he managed to clear up the new country's financial affairs, he improved relations with Great Britain and began the process of obtaining amicable treaties with the Native Americans. Washington also, by reluctantly accepting a second term as president, prevented the party factionalism of Thomas Jefferson and Alexander Hamilton from destroying the country.

2) Improving Quality of Life

    Washington lobbied for adoption of the Bill of Rights, the lack of which caused some states to reluctantly approve the Constitution, and slowed ratification by North Carolina and Rhode Island. Washington was a highly visible supporter of westward expansion, having been a speculator in western lands from pre-revolutionary times. He was a promoter of the Chesapeake and Ohio Canal, an early transportation improvement.

3) Meeting Crises

    Washington as president took the bull by the horns by severely crushing the Whiskey Rebellion, an early anti-tax revolt.

4) Overcoming Opposition

    Washington initially had no opposition, being unanimously elected in the Electoral College for both his terms as president. He did begin to face some opposition in his second term, when he began to side more often with Alexander Hamilton and the Federalists against Thomas Jefferson and the "Republicans".

Washington's rating:

CATEGORY	VALUE	RATING
1) Making America Great	10	90%
2) Improving Quality of Life	8	80%
3) Meeting Crises	10	90%
4) Overcoming Opposition	8	50%

Total rating: 28.4

2) Abraham Lincoln, Republican

Many people, regardless of their political affiliation, rank Abraham Lincoln as our greatest president, and a good case can be made for him as the greatest. Abraham Lincoln faced the greatest opposition to doing his job of any president, eleven states choosing to secede from the union rather than accept his presidency. He was a minority president in his first term, receiving only 45% of the popular vote and only being elected because the remainder of the popular vote was distributed among three other major candidates so that Lincoln had a plurality in most of the states that did not secede. Lincoln accomplished a great deal during his presidency; he initiated construction of the transcontinental railroad to tie the western states to the remainder of the country, and most significantly, he began the eradication of slavery. While Congress was Republican in both the House and Senate throughout Lincoln's presidency, the leaders of Congress strongly opposed Lincoln's conduct of the war and his policy of leniency toward the South.

While Lincoln was not originally in favor of forcing an end to slavery, this was how he was perceived by southerners, and secession was basically a ploy to avoid freeing of the slaves. The Civil War was originally fought, from the North's point of view, to "preserve the Union." This was not an abstract concept; the secession of the South essentially nullified the Louisiana Purchase. Arkansas, Louisiana, and Texas were on the west side of the Mississippi and the remainder of the Confederacy was on the east side, ending United States sovereignty at the southern borders of Missouri and Kentucky. Eventually Lincoln saw that he could not justify continuing the most destructive war yet seen unless it did promise the end of slavery, and issued his emancipation proclamations after two difficult years of war. The final Emancipation Proclamation also put an end to European, and most significantly, British, consideration of open support of the Confederacy.

The tragic irony of the Civil War is that it was unnecessary. Lincoln truly was not an abolitionist, and would have been content to allow slavery to continue in the then-existing slave states for as long as it was desired there by southern leaders. Lincoln believed that slavery would eventually die out, as it was not economically viable. The slave-based cultivation of cotton was barely self-sustaining, due to the extremely poor efficiency of slave labor. In addition, the slave population in the cotton-producing areas could not sustain itself, and cotton plantation owners relied on procurement of slaves from Maryland and Virginia when they could not get them internationally after the banning of the international slave trade. The eventual mechanization of the harvesting of cotton did away with the need for large amounts of unskilled labor, but this was decades away at the time of the Civil War. Without the need for their labor, there would be no need for plantation owners to support the slave population, and they would have presumably been freed voluntarily. The integration of the former slaves into southern society would be an entirely different matter.

Lincoln faced considerable opposition to going to war against the south except from the abolitionists who considered slavery a moral evil that justified using violence to end it. Most Northerners who welcomed the Civil War and supported it with their blood and treasure were primarily concerned with avoiding the spread of slavery into the West, and this was Lincoln's primary reason for running for president. Economically Lincoln was a Whig, and sat in Congress as a Whig from 1847-1849. Lincoln understood the value of the Mississippi River in the exporting of Midwestern crops and other products, having twice floated flatboats laden with commodities produced in the upper Midwest down to New Orleans for export. He may have seen Confederate control of the lower Mississippi River as it passed between the states of Mississippi and Arkansas, and through Louisiana, as justifying going to war. As he said after the Vicksburg campaign, "Now the Father of Waters goes unvexed to the sea."

A case could be made that Abraham Lincoln is the greatest man who became president of the United States. He rose from extremely humble surroundings, he faced severe personal difficulties, and he appeared to receive very little personal profit from his political activities.

Abraham Lincoln was a lawyer who was fully in tune with the commercial interests of the United States. His most remunerative court cases were in defending the emerging railroads of the country, particularly in the fast-growing Middle West, from restraints attempted by the opponents of the railroads. He was, to some extent, a speculator who expected to profit from his commercial decisions made as president. He owned property in Council Bluffs, Iowa, that was sure to increase in value when he deemed that the east end of the transcontinental railroad would be located there.

Regarding the qualities by which the presidents are evaluated, Lincoln fares as follows:

1) Making America Great

    By winning the Civil War, Lincoln established the Republican Party in control of the nation. The Republicans, while formed as an anti-slavery party, included the Whigs, who were in favor of increased national wealth with government assistance in the form of land grants for railroads and other internal improvements, a national bank to assure stable financing, and a permanent national debt to keep the financial community in harmony with the national government.

2) Improving Quality of Life

    By ending slavery, Lincoln removed a curse from the American landscape that thwarted the aspirations of people in all walks of life.

3) Meeting Crises

    Lincoln successfully met the worst peril that faced the United States, the secession of a key part of the country.

4) Overcoming Opposition

    Lincoln was initially a minority president, having won only a plurality of the electoral vote in his first election. He was considered little more than an amateur by the leaders of his own party and had to fight to achieve and maintain his leadership. He initially faced opposition for the nomination in 1864.

Lincoln's rating:

CATEGORY	VALUE	RATING
1) Making America Great	10	90%
2) Improving Quality of Life	8	55%
3) Meeting Crises	10	100%
4) Overcoming Opposition	8	60%

Total rating: 28.2

3) Ronald Reagan, Republican

Ronald Reagan accomplished what his seven immediate predecessors failed to do: end the Cold War. He also, perhaps coincidentally, began the recovery from the "stagflation" of the 1960s and 1970s that had reached a dangerously high level during the presidency of Jimmy Carter, the man Reagan replaced. Reagan never had a Republican Congress to work with him. The Senate was Republican in the 97th, 98th, and 99th Congresses, but the House of Representatives was held by the Democrats throughout Reagan's Presidency. Reagan was able, in spite of ideological differences, to establish a rapport with Congress; perhaps his Irish ancestry allowed him to find common ground with Tip O'Neil, the Irish-American congressman from Massachusetts who was Speaker of the House of Representatives during Reagan's Presidency. The special increase of immigration quotas for the Irish may have been a product of this meeting of the minds.

Ronald Reagan began his career as an actor, achieving mid-level stardom in several motion pictures that were fairly well regarded, but were not necessarily blockbusters. He rose to political prominence while an actor, becoming active in the liberal-leaning Screen Actor's Guild and was eventually its president. He switched from Democrat to Republican during the McCarthy Era of the late 1940s and early 1950s, when many members of the motion picture profession were found to be Communists or Communist sympathizers. He was one of the few politicians to successfully switch parties, perhaps because he did so before entering electoral politics on a national level. He went on to become a powerful governor of California before running for president.

Regarding the qualities by which the presidents are evaluated, Reagan fares as follows:

1) Making America Great

Ronald Reagan successfully moved the United States from the malaise following the embarrassments of the Nixon Administration and the incompetence of the Carter Administration, returning the United States to its position as the supreme World Power. Reagan successfully negotiated an arms limitations treaty with the Soviet Union. Reagan's adoption of confrontation and dismissal of détente was the key to the dissolution of the Soviet Union. Reagan proposed a Strategic Defense Initiative, dubbed "Star Wars" that would employ futuristic weapons in national defense.

2) Improving Quality of Life

Reagan's domestic policies returned the country to prosperity after several years of stagnation, partly by ending the excessive inflation that had neared 20% annually during the Carter Administration. While ending inflation Reagan saw millions of new jobs created in the United States economy and also oversaw tax reduction and income tax simplification. Reagan saw to reform of Social Security and Medicare, adding more people to the eligibility lists while increasing taxes to pay for the increased benefits, making the fund solvent for the first time in its history. Ronald Reagan appointed Sandra Day O'Connor to be the first woman on the United States Supreme Court.

3) Meeting Crises

Reagan successfully overcame the rumblings of the death throes of the Soviet Union, avoiding major disruption as the "Evil Empire" staggered toward dissolution. Reagan also spectacularly survived being wounded in an assassination attempt. The United States and its Western Allies withdrew from Lebanon in 1984 after failing to bring an end to hostilities between Israel and its Arab foes. Reagan became involved in the Iran-Contra scandal in 1986 but emerged relatively unscathed in spite of it becoming an embarrassment to the United States government.

4) Overcoming Opposition
Ronald Reagan was not taken seriously as a presidential candidate in spite of his success as governor of California. Opponents credited the successes of his administration to his staff, not to him, and continued to belittle his accomplishments through to the end of his presidency. Successfully, in the face of strenuous opposition, Reagan fired the nation's air traffic controllers after they began an illegal strike. After the United States Senate became controlled by the Democratic Party, Reagan was unable to get his conservative choices for Supreme Court Associate Justice confirmed, and had to settle for a moderate, Anthony M. Kennedy, who was confirmed without dispute.

Reagan's rating:

CATEGORY	VALUE	RATING
1) Making America Great	10	80%
2) Improving Quality of Life	8	80%
3) Meeting Crises	10	80%
4) Overcoming Opposition	8	60%

Total rating: 27.2

CHAPTER 6 — THE VERY GOOD PRESIDENTS

Several Presidents accomplished great things, but there were also failures in their administrations, or activities or events that were detrimental, but not enough so to balance out their major achievements.

4) Thomas Jefferson, "Republican"*

Thomas Jefferson accomplished one thing that assured his place as one of our greatest presidents: He purchased the Louisiana territory from France, covering the entire western Mississippi River Basin, from New Orleans to the Rocky Mountains, in spite of having grave doubts as to having the legal authority to do so. He was, thankfully in this case, the first of many presidents to change his political philosophy in the face of immense potential gain. Jefferson was the first of nine Democrat (although his party was called "Republican" at the time) presidents to have a Congress fully in sympathy with him throughout his presidency.

Jefferson was one of the most liberal of the Founding Fathers and was rather skeptical of the Constitution adopted in 1788. He was very much in sympathy with the French Revolution as he felt it to be very much an expression of the democratic ideals of the people. Jefferson might be considered one of the original "bleeding heart liberals" but taken within the context of his times his heart did not bleed that much. Jefferson is often mistakenly credited with originating the expression, "that government is best which governs the least" (see page 35). He did, however, evolve from his strict states-rights, limited Federal government position to becoming something of a nationalist after

---

*The party of Thomas Jefferson, not the party of Abraham Lincoln.

attaining the Presidency and coming face-to-face with the job of governing within the constraints of a strict Constitution.

Jefferson was a more than partisan politician. He was more than willing to use extralegal means to destroy or at least confound his enemies. He manipulated the treason trial of Aaron Burr in a desperate attempt to get a conviction, but failed. Jefferson attempted to bring Napoleon and the British Empire to bay during the Napoleonic Wars by his Embargo Act, but succeeded only in causing suffering among American farmers and producers of other goods who were unable to export their products except by smuggling, mostly by overland transport, which became rife.

Regarding the qualities by which the presidents are evaluated, Jefferson fares as follows:

1) Making America Great
   Jefferson's Louisiana Purchase, made in spite of his misgivings about the constitutionality of the move, doubled the size of the United States, making it a nation to be reckoned with on the international scene.

2) Improving Quality of Life
   The original purpose of the Louisiana Purchase was to obtain the Port of New Orleans for the benefit of farmers in the American West. This was admirably achieved, allowing the west to prosper and giving all Americans an opportunity to "go west," even within the original boundaries of the United States, and achieve their destiny.

3) Meeting Crises
   Jefferson did not fare so well in international relations, becoming something of a tool of Napoleon in his battle with the British. Following his principles, he reduced the size of the United States government, including the army, navy, and diplomatic service, at a time when all were needed in the tempestuous international situation.

4) Overcoming Opposition
   Jefferson had little domestic opposition during his presidency. The

Federalist Party was on the wane, and Jefferson's distaste for the antics of Aaron Burr was shared by many of his fellow citizens, of both parties. Jefferson immediately, upon assuming the presidency, freed all political prisoners arrested by the Federalists under the Alien and Sedition Acts.

Jefferson's rating:

CATEGORY	VALUE	RATING
1) Making America Great	10	100%
2) Improving Quality of Life	8	70%
3) Meeting Crises	10	60%
4) Overcoming Opposition	8	50%

Total rating: 25.6

5) John Adams, Federalist

John Adams appointed John Marshall to the Supreme Court, setting that body on its way to become an equal and important third branch of the Federal government. Adams also was the father of the United States Navy. By creating a permanent Navy, and successfully thwarting the aims of France in the XYZ affair, Adams assured that the United States received the respect it deserved in the eyes of the rest of the world. The House of Representatives and the Senate were both Federalist throughout Adams' single term as president, the last time that party would have significant power on the national scene.

John Adams, in spite of being one of the strongest advocates of revolution and independence, became a strong proponent of alliance with Britain after independence was achieved, a position shared by most of his Federalist colleagues.

Regarding the qualities by which the presidents are evaluated, John Adams fares as follows:

1) Making America Great

John Adams made the Navy a permanent part of the United States' defense establishment. Adams successfully ended the XYZ affair, thwarting the attempt by France to control American foreign policy.

As part of preparation for war with France over the affair, Adams called George Washington back to active duty as head of the army; unfortunately Adams and the Federalists also put into law, in reaction to the threat of war, what were called the Alien and Sedition Acts, severely curtailing the Bill of Rights. Eventually, Adams sent commissioners to France and ended the war scare.

2) Improving Quality of Life
Adams appointed many competent and distinguished men to the courts of the United States, including making John Marshall the Chief Justice of the Supreme Court, helping to assure that the United States would be a country under the rule of law.

3) Meeting Crises
As mentioned above, John Adams successfully resolved the XYZ affair.

4) Overcoming Opposition
Adams was not a personable politician, and had difficulty in personal relationships. He was an opponent of the more extreme followers of fellow Federalist Alexander Hamilton, who were largely in control of the Federalist Party. In spite of this, Adams was generally successful in all he attempted to do as president

Adams' rating:

CATEGORY	VALUE	RATING
1) Making America Great	10	70%
2) Improving Quality of Life	8	70%
3) Meeting Crises	10	70%
4) Overcoming Opposition	8	70%
Total rating: 25.2		

6) James K. Polk, Democrat

James Knox Polk assured the fulfillment of America's "Manifest Destiny" by adding Oregon and the Great Southwest to the territory of the United

States. The fact that he did so primarily to add more slave states to the Union is irrelevant, as what territory was gained by the Mexican War ended up as free states: California before the Civil War, Nevada before the end of the Civil War; Colorado, Utah, Oklahoma, New Mexico, and Arizona after the Civil War. Concurrently with the Mexican War, Polk negotiated a treaty with what is now Colombia to allow the United States to build a railway or canal across the Panamanian isthmus. Polk started with a Democrat Congress but the House turned Whig in the 30th Congress.

James K. Polk was not a popular politician, and only was nominated as a presidential candidate after his Democratic Party could not agree on a choice between the more prominent members of the party.

Regarding the qualities by which the presidents are evaluated, Polk fares as follows:

1) Making America Great
   James K. Polk was the most energetic and enthusiastic of all the expansionist presidents. His primary motive was the expansion of slavery, but none of the territory acquired by the United States during his presidency, except Texas, which was already on the path to statehood before Polk took office, became slave territory, slave states, or part of the Confederacy. With Oregon and the Southwest, Polk added more territory to the United States than the Louisiana or Alaska purchases.

2) Improving Quality of Life
   Polk's aggressive capture of California greatly increased the wealth of the United States, especially after the discovery of gold in 1848. This increased the money supply, allowing economic expansion, as well as providing opportunities for hundreds of thousands of people in the new mining frontier.

3) Meeting Crises
   While it could be said that Polk created the crises he successfully overcame, nevertheless many Americans who emigrated to Texas welcomed the intervention of the United States in their struggle against Mexican government oppression.

4) Overcoming Opposition

Polk had little domestic opposition to his policies. Some felt he was not as aggressive in his efforts to obtain Oregon as he was in going after Texas and the Southwest, but the only real opposition to his policies was from some of the same Easterners who objected to the Louisiana Purchase on the grounds that it diluted their influence in Washington.

Polk's rating:

CATEGORY	VALUE	RATING
1) Making America Great	10	90%
2) Improving Quality of Life	8	60%
3) Meeting Crises	10	70%
4) Overcoming Opposition	8	50%

Total rating: 24.8

7) Theodore Roosevelt, Republican

Theodore Roosevelt was America's first progressive president, and ran under the progressive, "Bull Moose" banner in 1912 after he served the remainder of the assassinated McKinley's second term and his own 4-year presidential term, and after one term by his anointed successor, William Howard Taft. Theodore Roosevelt was a Republican throughout his presidency, and had a Republican Congress for the whole time he was president.

Theodore Roosevelt was responsible for construction of the Panama Canal by the United States. While his means of doing this caused some unfavorable feeling among the nations of Latin America, it improved the prestige of the United States in the world at large. It also helped the defense posture of the United States by easing communication between the East, Atlantic coast and the West, Pacific coast of the United States. Improved water transportation between the east and west coasts also helped reduce the effective monopoly that railroads had in freight transportation in the United States.

Theodore Roosevelt was one of the most popular politicians to hold the office of president, and surely could have been reelected to as many terms as he chose to serve if he had not stepped down in 1908. It is fairly certain that he regretted his announcement that he would not run for another term as president in 1908 almost as soon as he made the announcement. He was a very ambitious person who wanted very much to be in charge of things. His "New Nationalism" placed the federal government as supreme over state and individual rights, contrary to the 9th and 10th Amendments. This did not bother most people as they saw "TR" as fighting for them against the "Establishment" and the "Robber Barons."

Regarding the qualities by which the presidents are evaluated, Theodore Roosevelt fares as follows:

1) Making America Great

   By initiating the successful construction of the Panama Canal, even though by assisting in the creation of a revolution in Colombia leading to independence for Panama, Theodore Roosevelt placed the United States among the first rank of world powers. His sending of the Great White Fleet on world tour advertised the fact. His Roosevelt Corollary to the Monroe Doctrine cemented the position of the United States as leader of the Western Hemisphere nations. Theodore Roosevelt's arbitration of the Russo-Japanese War earned him the Nobel Peace Prize.

2) Improving Quality of Life

   Theodore Roosevelt successfully brought the biggest of the big businessmen of the United States to understand that they were answerable to the government and people of the United States for their actions. He intervened in the 1902 strike of the anthracite coal miners, on the side of the miners, forcing the coal mine owners to enter into arbitration to end the strike. Roosevelt pressured Congress to pass the Hepburn Act, strengthening regulation of the railroads of the United States, in 1906.

3) Meeting Crises

   Theodore Roosevelt was not as aggressive a trust-buster as he was sometimes portrayed. By maintaining a relationship with J.P. Morgan and other financiers of the era, Roosevelt kept the Panic of 1907 from being a serious drag on the economy.

4) Overcoming Opposition

Theodore Roosevelt was an extremely popular president, with his only serious opposition coming from the leaders of the great trusts that he was endeavoring to keep under control. This opposition manifested itself in the refusal of the Republican Party to nominate him for president in 1912, even though it was apparent that the incumbent, Taft, would likely come in third if Roosevelt ran as an independent or third-party candidate in that election and the Democrats nominated a progressive candidate.

Theodore Roosevelt's rating:

CATEGORY	VALUE	RATING
1) Making America Great	10	80%
2) Improving Quality of Life	8	80%
3) Meeting Crises	10	60%
4) Overcoming Opposition	8	50%

Total rating: 24.4

CHAPTER 7 – THE BETTER-THAN-AVERAGE PRESIDENTS

Many presidents served out their terms while making modest improvements in the state of the union and not doing anything detrimental; others, such as Richard Nixon, combined great accomplishments with disasters.

8) Dwight Eisenhower, Republican

Eisenhower was perhaps the epitome of the middle-of-the-road presidents; he was also, perhaps, the closest to a non-partisan statesman of any president since Washington. As a retired general, Eisenhower was pursued by both major political parties to be their candidate in the 1952 presidential election. Eisenhower chose the Republicans as he felt their party philosophy to be more in tune with that of Middle America. Eisenhower had a Republican 83rd Congress but thereafter both the House and Senate were controlled by the Democrats.

Dwight Eisenhower was responsible for initiating construction of the Interstate Highway system in the United States, making it much easier for Americans to travel within the country. His interest in highways dated from his early army experience in participating in a cross-country convoy of army vehicles shortly after World War I. He may have also gotten a bit of anti-railroad attitude from his father, a blue-collar railroad employee, and may have been interested in loosening the railroads' grip on the long-distance freight business. The Interstate Highways also improved the distribution of consumer goods throughout the United States.

Eisenhower rose swiftly from relative obscurity to be the leader of the World War II allied forces fighting Nazi Germany. He was considered a Far Eastern expert prior to World War II, but had little to do with the defeat of totalitarian Japan. He continued to demonstrate his administrative and diplomatic abilities after the war as a college president and as the head of the North Atlantic Treaty Organization. He appeared to be of a somewhat liberal turn politically, but when both major parties in the United States asked him to be their presidential candidate in 1952 he chose the Republicans.

Regarding the qualities by which the presidents are evaluated, Eisenhower fares as follows:

1) Making America Great

   As president, Eisenhower demonstrated leadership on the international scene responding to crises in Southeast Asia and the Middle East. He attended a summit meeting with the leaders of Great Britain, France, and Russia, although it accomplished little. He went to the United Nations where he called for planning for the peaceful use of atomic energy, leading to formation of the International Atomic Energy Agency. Eisenhower condemned the United Kingdom and France for their heavy-handed handling of the Suez Crisis. Continuing past United States policy, he failed to assist the Hungarians in their uprising against the Russian-backed Hungarian communists. After receiving congressional approval, he promulgated what was to be called the "Eisenhower Doctrine," offering assistance to countries requesting assistance against armed aggression by international communism. This led to military intervention in Lebanon and Taiwan. But Cuba was lost to communism under Eisenhower's watch.

2) Improving Quality of Life

   Eisenhower's stewardship in promoting the Interstate Highway system gave Americans greater ease of travel and more expeditious delivery of consumer goods. Eisenhower expanded Social Security, increased the minimum wage – to $1 per hour! - and began the desegregation of schools in the United States, using federal troops to help integration in the South. In his farewell address, Eisenhower warned the people of America to beware of undue influence by the military-industrial complex.

3) Meeting Crises

Eisenhower managed to dodge a bullet when a U-2 spy plane pilot was downed inside the Soviet Union. This event did cause the cancellation of a summit conference between Eisenhower and Soviet Premier Nikita Khrushchev.

4) Overcoming Opposition

Eisenhower had little opposition during his two presidential terms, although some pundits felt that he was a figurehead and that others were actually running the government.

Eisenhower's rating:

CATEGORY	VALUE	RATING
1) Making America Great	10	70%
2) Improving Quality of Life	8	80%
3) Meeting Crises	10	60%
4) Overcoming Opposition	8	50%

Total rating: 23.4

9) Richard M Nixon, Republican

In a popularity contest (see Chapters 12-14), Richard Nixon would have, at the end of his presidency, come in close to dead last. His reputation improved somewhat as time went on, but he is still viewed unfavorably by most people. Not so in 1968, when, even a year before the election, polls showed Nixon to be more popular than Lyndon Johnson, or at least less unpopular. Both the House and Senate were held by the Democrats throughout Nixon's presidency. In the 1968 Presidential Election, Nixon had the advantage of George Wallace running as a third party candidate. Wallace's far right position made Nixon seem to be a middle-of-the-roader when compared to ultraliberal, for the time, Hubert Humphrey, the Democratic Party candidate. Richard Nixon probably had more to do with the improvement in the quality of life within the United States than any other president, by his encouraging the creation of the Environmental Protection Agency under his watch. The EPA has had a profound effect on the quality of air and water within the United States.

In international relations, Nixon's visit to Communist China while president had a major effect on the international balance of power, greatly improving the status of the United States internationally. It also pushed the Soviet Union into a more defensive stance, leading eventually to its dissolution.

Richard Nixon would probably have been impeached and removed from office in the wake of the Watergate scandal if he had not resigned. His arrogant disregard for political realities in the 1972 election campaign caused him the loss of support of many within his own party as well as people and political operatives in general. His many beneficial acts were completely ignored once it became apparent to most people that he had had a personal hand in the Watergate break-in. With both houses of Congress firmly in the hand of the opposition party, Nixon's impeachment and removal from office was highly likely, although an escape as per Andrew Johnson was not impossible; Nixon's resignation made it moot.

Regarding the qualities by which the presidents are evaluated, Nixon fares as follows:

1) Making America Great
   Richard Nixon effectively broke the close bonds between the Union of Soviet Socialist Republics and the People's Republic of China, putting the United States in sole first place among the world's powers. Nixon's administration had the good fortune to be in place during the culmination of the United States space program when Neil Armstrong and Edwin Aldrin landed on the Moon in July of 1969.

2) Improving Quality of Life
   The creation of the Environmental Protection Agency under Nixon's watch brought about an immediate improvement in the air and water that people of the United States had to breathe and drink. Nixon also pursued improvements in urban life that had been initiated previously.

3) Meeting Crises
   Nixon held his own during several international incidents, but his handling of the Watergate scandal completely negated his performance in

other arenas. The United States Supreme Court entered an era of controversy when Lyndon Johnson attempted to place Abe Fortas as Chief Justice. Fortas' confirmation process became drawn out, and he had to withdraw his name when irregularities in his past surfaced. Nixon ended up nominating Warren Burger as Chief Justice, and Burger was quickly confirmed. Eventually Nixon named two associate justices to the Supreme Court, resulting in the first conservative Supreme Court majority since the beginning of the Franklin Roosevelt Administration.

4) Overcoming Opposition

Nixon narrowly lost the presidential election of 1960. In spite of likely voter fraud in Illinois and Texas, whereby John F. Kennedy narrowly won the general election, Nixon chose not to pursue a recount, even though there was evidence of systemic corruption in the Kennedy campaign, going back to the Democratic Party nomination process. Nixon's sending of United States troops into Cambodia, expanding the Viet Nam war, caused his popularity to plummet. The killing of protesters and bystanders by National Guard troops at Kent State University in Ohio quickly turned public opinion in the United States against the war. Nixon's Cambodian venture resulted in Congress passing a war powers act over Nixon's veto, limiting the president's ability to engage in military activity without Congressional approval. Accomplishing what he did during his presidency in spite of being almost completely hamstrung during his second administration is testimony to Richard Nixon's ability to overcome opposition.

Nixon's rating:

CATEGORY	VALUE	RATING
1) Making America Great	10	70%
2) Improving Quality of Life	8	80%
3) Meeting Crises	10	50%
4) Overcoming Opposition	8	60%

Total rating: 23.2

10) George H. W. Bush, Republican

George Herbert Walker Bush's primary legacy as president was his continuation of the policies of Ronald Reagan, resulting in the dissolution of the Union of Soviet Socialist Republics in December of 1991. The end of the Soviet Union meant less ideological tension in Europe and elsewhere in the world, improving the quality of life everywhere. Like Reagan, George Herbert Walker Bush faced a Democrat-controlled Congress throughout his presidency.

George Herbert Walker Bush was the utilitarian president. He had served a variety of jobs in the government before winning election to the nation's highest office in 1988. G. H. W. Bush served in all but the judicial branches of government; starting as a congressman, he served in a variety of executive positions: Head of the Central Intelligence Agency, Ambassador to the United Nations, eventually vice president.

Regarding the qualities by which the presidents are evaluated, George H.W. Bush fares as follows:

1) Making America Great

    George H. W. Bush continued the pressure on the Soviet Union, eventually witnessing its dissolution. He successfully led an international coalition that expelled Iraq from Kuwait (and obtained for himself a 90% approval rating by the American public).

2) Improving Quality of Life

    George H. W. Bush presided over the continuing improvement in prosperity for the American people. He strongly supported free trade in North America between Canada, Mexico, and the United States, and made efforts to prepare the United States for increased economic globalization.

3) Meeting Crises

    George H. W. Bush successfully led the coalition that removed Iraq, which had invaded under the leadership of Saddam Hussein, from Kuwait. George H.W. Bush steadfastly maintained a friendly stance toward Chinese leaders in spite of increased Chinese government oppression against their own people.

4) Overcoming Opposition

In spite of dealing with a Congress increasingly controlled by the Democratic Party, George H. W. Bush had little opposition for the first part of his term, but lost the confidence of the majority of the American people by the end of his term. He became one of the few American presidents to have been elected to office and then lose his bid for a second term.

George Herbert Walker Bush's rating:

CATEGORY	VALUE	RATING
1) Making America Great	10	65%
2) Improving Quality of Life	8	60%
3) Meeting Crises	10	60%
4) Overcoming Opposition	8	60%

Total rating: 22.1

11) Chester A. Arthur, Republican

Chester A. Arthur was known as a political hack until he became president. The assassination of James A. Garfield by a self-proclaimed political spoils seeker greatly chastened Arthur, and turned him into an advocate of political reform in Washington. Specifically, Arthur promoted reform in the civil service, signing the Pendleton Act that took politics out of much of the civil service in the federal government. Either the Senate or the House of Representatives was under Democrat opposition control throughout Arthur's presidency.

In spite of his surprisingly competent performance as president, Arthur was refused the opportunity by his party to run for a full term of his own.

Regarding the qualities by which the presidents are evaluated, Arthur fares as follows:

1) Making America Great

Arthur continued the advancement of the United States into prominence in world affairs. He attempted to keep Congress from enacting an extremely high protective tariff. Arthur proposed an agreement of

Western Hemisphere countries to prevent war, and to unite in a common currency to improve trade.

2) Improving Quality of Life

Arthur took steps to rein in the spoils system, which dated from the Jackson Administration, that hampered good government in Washington by turning most government employees out into the street whenever the Administration changed. Arthur was instrumental in adopting Standard Time in the United States. He attempted to get the United States Senate to approve a treaty with Nicaragua to construct an Atlantic-Pacific canal. Arthur proposed federal aid to education, a radical idea at the time, and proposed clarifying the rules on presidential succession.

3) Meeting Crises

Little of moment occurred during Arthur's administration (except for the assassination of Garfield that initiated his presidency). He vetoed some pork-barrel measures, but was overruled by Congress.

4) Overcoming Opposition

Arthur overcame disdain on the part of others in government, due to his previous reputation as a party hack, to take a leadership role in reforming the government in Washington.

Arthur's rating:

CATEGORY	VALUE	RATING
1) Making America Great	10	70%
2) Improving Quality of Life	8	55%
3) Meeting Crises	10	50%
4) Overcoming Opposition	8	70%
Total rating: 22.0		

12) William McKinley, Republican

William McKinley allowed the United States to become an imperial nation, by fighting the Spanish-American War and by annexing Hawaii. The Spanish-American War was not without its domestic opposition within the United States and elsewhere, and with the people in the territories involved. Cuba became a free country, as did the Philippines, while the people of Puerto Rico chose to remain a territory under the protection of the United States. Congress was controlled by the Republicans throughout McKinley's presidency. Party leadership was centered elsewhere than in the Executive Mansion while McKinley was president, but he received credit for most of the positive results of efforts in Washington during his presidency, primarily because of his success in working with Congress. McKinley was regarded by some as a figurehead, with Mark Hanna, a prominent Republican industrialist, considered to be his handler.

Regarding the qualities by which the presidents are evaluated, McKinley fares as follows:

1) Making America Great

    McKinley presided over the annexation of Hawaii and the victory over Spain in the Spanish-American War. He thus placed the United States squarely in the world-power camp and thwarted, at least temporarily, the isolationists of the U.S. McKinley had United States troops participate in putting down the Boxer Rebellion in China, but did so in such a way as to gain the appreciation of the Chinese people.

2) Improving Quality of Life

    Under McKinley's watch, industrialization in the United States took a major step forward, thanks to increased protective tariffs and a return to the gold standard, providing increased prosperity for most Americans. McKinley's substantial victory over William Jennings Bryan in the election of 1896, and his repeat victory in 1900 by a larger margin, effectively ended the cheap money campaign of the populists and kept the United States on a prosperous road. The overall wealth of the United States and its citizens reached, by the end of the McKinley Administration, perhaps its greatest level, relatively speaking, of any time in the history of the Republic

3) Meeting Crises

The gold crisis, with William Jennings Bryan campaigning for president, was an extremely volatile issue in the 1890s. McKinley and the Republicans successfully thwarted Bryan and his followers.

4) Overcoming Opposition

McKinley had little trouble overcoming opposition from the Left during his administration.

McKinley's rating:

CATEGORY	VALUE	RATING
1) Making America Great	10	70%
2) Improving Quality of Life	8	65%
3) Meeting Crises	10	55%
4) Overcoming Opposition	8	50%

Total rating: 21.7

13) William Howard Taft, Republican

William Howard Taft was a lawyer before becoming a public servant. Not unlike a later president, George H.W. Bush, Taft served in a variety of roles, particularly under Theodore Roosevelt, who endorsed Taft as his successor in 1908. The Republican Party controlled Congress during Taft's first two years in office, but as the Democrats began to jump onto the Progressive bandwagon the House and then the Senate became Democrat in the 62nd Congress.

Of a judicial turn of mind, Taft was happy to be appointed Chief Justice of the United States Supreme Court by Warren Harding.

Regarding the qualities by which the presidents are evaluated, Taft fares as follows:

1) Making America Great

Before becoming president, William Howard Taft negotiated agreements with the Philippines and with Cuba. He later supported the

League of Nations, with reservations. He strengthened the position of the United States regarding overseas colonies.

2) Improving Quality of Life
Taft was a true progressive. He drafted the constitutional amendment providing for direct election of senators and for the income tax. He continued, and expanded, the trust-control activities of his predecessor, Theodore Roosevelt. Taft, while president, proposed banking and currency reform that later led to the Federal Reserve System.

3) Meeting Crises
Taft had little in the way of crises to contend with during his administration.

4) Overcoming Opposition
Taft was a progressive, but many felt that he was not aggressive enough in his pursuance of progressive policies. As the Republican candidate, he ran a distant third behind Woodrow Wilson and Theodore Roosevelt in his reelection attempt in 1912.

Taft's rating:

CATEGORY	VALUE	RATING
1) Making America Great	10	75%
2) Improving Quality of Life	8	70%
3) Meeting Crises	10	50%
4) Overcoming Opposition	8	40%

Total rating: 21.3

14) Herbert Hoover, Republican

Herbert Clark Hoover was perhaps the greatest humanitarian to have served as president. Herbert Hoover had made a fortune as a mining engineer and businessman, and devoted his later life to public service. He took the responsibility to manage the distribution of food and other necessities to refugees in

Belgium and other areas of Europe during and after World War I. Unfortunately for him, he was President of the United States when the stock market crashed in October of 1929. While he initiated many of the most important programs used to combat the depression, many felt he did not provide sufficient sympathy to those suffering from the ravages of the Depression, and he was ignored by Congress after 1930. Hoover was inaugurated with a Republican Congress, but the House turned Democrat in the 72nd Congress in 1931.

Regarding the qualities by which the presidents are evaluated, Hoover fares as follows:

1) Making America Great

   Hoover took a leading role in international attempts to mitigate the effects of the depression that began in 1929.

2) Improving Quality of Life

   Hoover initiated most of the key federal government programs that were put into effect to ease the hardships suffered by the American people during the Great Depression. Hoover called for and received from Congress an income tax cut, and he initiated several public works programs.

3) Meeting Crises

   Hoover was internationally famous as the person who led the relief efforts to help the Belgian people during and after World War I. He did not perform similar duties for the American people as the depression of the 1930s deepened, but did initiate federal programs to provide funding to provide useful work for the unemployed.

4) Overcoming Opposition

   In spite of a complete lack of cooperation by Congress, Hoover was able to initiate some programs to ease the effects of the Great Depression.

Hoover's rating:

CATEGORY	VALUE	RATING
1) Making America Great	10	50%
2) Improving Quality of Life	8	35%
3) Meeting Crises	10	75%
4) Overcoming Opposition	8	70%

Total rating: 20.9

15) Calvin Coolidge, Republican

Calvin Coolidge was one of the most disparaged presidents, perhaps because of his taciturn ways and seeming lack of humor. This was a misapprehension, as those who know of his response to the woman who bet she could get him to say more than three words ("you lose") are well aware. Coolidge also famously posed, while president, in an Indian chief's headdress while on vacation in South Dakota. The House of Representatives and the Senate were Republican throughout Coolidge's presidency. Coolidge was the first vice president to regularly sit in on Cabinet meetings, perhaps because of Harding's lack of confidence in his own leadership qualities. He was firmly in the capitalist camp while "Red Scares" were causing concern around the country. He famously said "The chief business of America is business".*

Regarding the qualities by which the presidents are evaluated, Coolidge fares as follows:

1) Making America Great

   Coolidge restored the respect of the United States worldwide after the scandals of the Harding Administration came to light. Coolidge famously refused to ease off on demanding that the Allies of World War I repay their war debts to the United States: "They hired the money, didn't they?" Coolidge's Secretary of State, Frank Kellogg, won the 1929 Nobel Peace Prize for negotiating the Kellogg-Briand Pact outlawing war.

---

*In an address to Society of American Newspaper Editors on January 17, 1925

2) Improving Quality of Life
    Coolidge did what he could to stabilize the economy during the heady days of the roaring twenties: He reduced the national debt and vetoed spending bills, some of which were passed by Congress over his veto.

3) Meeting Crises
    Coolidge successfully weathered the exposure of the Teapot Dome and Elk Hills scandals but he chose to retire rather than deal with the dangerous financial situation that was looming and led to the Great Depression.

4) Overcoming Opposition
    Coolidge had no significant political opposition as president. He easily won the election of 1924 even though there was a Progressive Party candidate (Robert M. La Follette) in the field who won some electoral votes. Presumably, he could have easily obtained the Republican nomination in 1928 if he had chosen to run. In Washington, Coolidge faced a formidable opposition consisting of Democrats and Republican progressives.

Coolidge's rating:

CATEGORY	VALUE	RATING
1) Making America Great	10	70%
2) Improving Quality of Life	8	70%
3) Meeting Crises	10	50%
4) Overcoming Opposition	8	40%

Total rating: 20.8

16) Gerald R Ford, Republican

Gerald Ford had the unenviable task of cleaning up the mess after Richard Nixon's resignation in 1974. He was somewhat handicapped by being the only president who was never elected president or vice president, but he and his family became quite popular as residents of the White House. His popularity was insufficient to overcome several public gaffes, as well as the controversial pardoning of Richard Nixon, and he narrowly lost the 1976 presidential election to Jimmy Carter, 240 to 297 in the Electoral College (39,148,940 to 40,828,929; by 2.1% in the popular vote). Ford inherited Nixon's Democrat-controlled Congress.

Regarding the qualities by which the presidents are evaluated, Ford fares as follows:

1) Making America Great
   Gerald Ford had a reputation as a competent member of the House of Representatives in foreign affairs and was able to maintain the status of the United States internationally after the Watergate debacle. Ford met in 1975 in Helsinki, Finland, with leaders of the Soviet Union and more than thirty other countries to sign an agreement guaranteeing the boundaries of European countries and providing security of human rights for residents of all the countries signing the agreement.

2) Improving Quality of Life
   Ford's pardon of Richard Nixon and provisional amnesty to Viet Nam War protesters resolved issues that were tormenting the United States internally, although Ford was criticized roundly from all sides for his actions. Economic difficulties were endemic throughout the 1970s and 1980s, largely stemming from the Arab oil embargo and resulting high energy prices, with chronic inflation and simultaneous recession and high unemployment; Ford's economic policies and attempts to reduce dependence on foreign oil slowed inflation but were largely responsible for the recession that grew to near-depression levels before the end of Ford's presidency.

3) Meeting Crises
   Ford's attempts to respond to the North Vietnamese breaking of the truce were ignored by Congress, resulting in the fall of governments in South Viet Nam, Laos, and Cambodia. Ford's attempts to negotiate a further arms reduction treaty were hampered by his dwindling popularity that made it unlikely he would be reelected in 1976.

4) Overcoming Opposition
While initially having the support of almost everyone, in the general population as well as in Washington, in his task of rescuing the presidency, by the end of his term Ford was ignored or shunned by almost all, resulting in a further weakening of the presidential office.

Ford's rating:

CATEGORY	VALUE	RATING
1) Making America Great	10	65%
2) Improving Quality of Life	8	65%
3) Meeting Crises	10	55%
4) Overcoming Opposition	8	40%

Total rating: 20.4

17) James Monroe, "Republican"*

James Monroe was president during the "Era of Good Feeling;" not so much an era of good feeling but the only period after the 18th century in the history of the United States when the United States was a single-party state. The Federalist Party had disappeared without its followers coming up with a new party, so that all serious politicians became members of the "Republican" Party, the then-current version of the Antifederalist Party, which eventually transmorphed (or transmogrified) into the Democratic Party. Monroe was an extremely popular president, in spite of being at the helm during the recession of 1819, the first major depression in the country's history. Congress was controlled by the "Republicans" (mostly former Antifederalists, later to be Democratic Republicans and then simply Democrats) throughout Monroe's presidency.

Regarding the qualities by which the presidents are evaluated, Monroe fares as follows:

---

*The party of Thomas Jefferson, not the party of Abraham Lincoln.

1) Making America Great
   Although most of the work was done by his secretary of state, John Quincy Adams, the Monroe Administration is famous for its clarification of issues in the Western Hemisphere. Monroe was responsible for treaties settling the boundary between the United States and British territories in North America, later the Dominion of Canada. In 1819, the United States acquired Florida from Spain. The Monroe Doctrine, stating that the New World was not to be considered territory for further European colonization, is still recognized today as part of international law respecting the rights of countries in Latin America.

2) Improving Quality of Life
   Monroe's presidency was generally considered as a period of peace, prosperity, and growth. During Monroe's administration, an agreement was made with Great Britain to eliminate fortifications along the United States – Canada border.

3) Meeting Crises
   There was little turmoil during the Monroe Administration, and no great crises to resolve.

4) Overcoming Opposition
   What was called "The Era of Good Feeling" was truly a period of immense popularity for the president, but it did not last long after he retired from office.

Monroe's rating:

CATEGORY	VALUE	RATING
1) Making America Great	10	60%
2) Improving Quality of Life	8	65%
3) Meeting Crises	10	50%
4) Overcoming Opposition	8	50%

Total rating: 20.2

18) John Quincy Adams, "Republican"*, later National Republican

John Quincy Adams was probably the unhappiest of all presidents. His career in government before and after his presidency, as Monroe's Secretary of State and as a Congressman, was much more fruitful and appreciated. John Quincy Adams won the presidency in the House of Representatives over Andrew Jackson, who had received the most popular and electoral votes in the election of 1824. Jackson did not receive a majority of the electoral vote, so that the election was decided in the House, for the second and, as of April 2020, the last time. Jackson's followers, not unlike the followers of the loser in every disputed election since, cried fraud loudly and long, making Adams' life miserable for the full length of his term. Jackson followers controlled the Senate and House of Representatives for all of Adams' single term, and made certain that Adams got absolutely none of his proposed programs through Congress. At the beginning of his presidency, John Quincy Adams was a "Republican", or Democratic Republican as they were later called. When the "Republican" Party shortly split up over the violent disagreements between the Adams followers and the followers of Jackson, Adams became a National Republican while Congress remained "Republican", but most "Republican" Party members considered themselves Jacksonians. These Jacksonians eventually renamed their party the Democratic Party.

Regarding the qualities by which the presidents are evaluated, John Quincy Adams fares as follows:

1) Making America Great
    Adams continued the strong foreign policies he advocated as Secretary of State under James Monroe, but had little opportunity for accomplishing anything concrete during his presidency.

2) Improving Quality of Life
    John Quincy Adams was the first president to be a strong advocate of internal improvements, with the goal of increasing the wealth of the country. He lifted the first shovel of earth in the construction of the Chesapeake and Ohio Canal.

---

*The party of Thomas Jefferson, not the party of Abraham Lincoln.

While canals proved to be not as effective in improving transportation facilities as would be the railroads that were first coming into use during Adams' presidential term, his promotion of internal improvements in spite of refusal of funding by a Democratic Congress, was of benefit to the young country.

3) Meeting Crises
Other than political opposition to his policies, John Quincy Adams faced no real crises during his administration.

4) Overcoming Opposition
Adams had a great deal of political opposition, as has been noted. He was not successful in overcoming it. What accomplishments he made were a result of his executive powers, not his political leadership.

John Quincy Adams' rating:

CATEGORY	VALUE	RATING
1) Making America Great	10	50%
2) Improving Quality of Life	8	65%
3) Meeting Crises	10	50%
4) Overcoming Opposition	8	50%

Total rating: 19.2

19) Zachary Taylor, Whig

Zachary Taylor was a hero of the Mexican War, who did not receive a majority of the popular vote in the Election of 1848 but did have a comfortable plurality over Lewis Cass, the Democrat Candidate, and Martin Van Buren, the Free-Soil Party candidate (presumably, Van Buren assured the election of Taylor by splitting the New York vote, as his votes (he was a former Democrat) supposedly would have gone to Cass, giving Cass New York's electoral votes and the election). Not much was expected of Taylor as president, as most of the major issues of the day seemed insoluble and he had no record in politics, but Taylor boldly stated his solutions to slavery extension and other issues. He stepped on many toes and died before implementing his proposed program. His death remains a mystery today, although some still believe he was poisoned, murdered by opponents of the restriction of slavery. In spite of being a southerner and a slaveholder, Taylor favored the Whig program of a protective tariff to encourage domestic manufactures. He also proposed setting up an Agriculture Bureau to aid farmers, and was a zealous advocate of a transcontinental railroad; both measures were enacted during the Lincoln Administration after the southern states seceded and the Democrats lost control of Congress.

Regarding the qualities by which the presidents are evaluated, Taylor fares as follows:

1) Making America Great

   Taylor was instrumental in winning the Mexican War with his overwhelming victories. His Whig politics earned him the enmity of President James K. Polk, and Polk used his position as Commander-in-Chief to keep Taylor out of as much of the final victory in the war as possible. Taylor worked strongly to make California the 31st state, in spite of the slavocracy's unwillingness to admit another free state. California, as a free state, was admitted to the union as the 31st state on September 9, 1850, just two months after Taylor's death. The entry of California permanently ended the parity between slave and free states in the Senate, probably making secession and the Civil War inevitable as the South saw itself becoming a minority member of the Union.

2) Improving Quality of Life

   Taylor opposed the Compromise of 1850, believing it to be too pro-slavery. His death in office allowed the Compromise to be enacted. If Taylor had not died, the Civil War probably would have been fought 10 years earlier, and probably would have resulted in a quicker Union victory with fewer casualties and less destruction. This could have meant a better reconstruction settlement with less long-term rancor and a possibility of better future racial harmony. Unfortunately, due to events, this is only speculation.

3) Meeting Crises

   The slaveholding South was on its way to permanently controlling the federal government when Taylor was elected. Taylor was faced with a Democrat Congress that was favorable to the extension of slavery as a means of avoiding civil war.

4) Overcoming Opposition
Taylor brooked no opposition to his policies, stating that he was clearly prepared to use the army to end treason when southerners were preparing to take over New Mexico and install slavery there by force. His death ended his efforts as Fillmore, his vice-president, took a more moderate position when moving into the Oval Office.

Taylor's rating:

CATEGORY	VALUE	RATING
1) Making America Great	10	60%
2) Improving Quality of Life	8	60%
3) Meeting Crises	10	50%
4) Overcoming Opposition	8	40%

Total rating: 19.0

20) Rutherford B Hayes, Republican

Hayes hobbled himself in the presidency by immediately announcing he would serve only one term. Single term presidencies had been the norm for a period before the Civil War, but with the reduction in presidential power after the assassination of Abraham Lincoln, Congress was able to overpower a president with limited ability to dole out patronage. Hayes apparently thought this was a good idea, as he proposed a single six-year term for the president, assuring permanent lame-duck status with all that that implied. Ironically, Hayes was a promoter of the civil service reform, although it did not take place until after his presidency.

Regarding the qualities by which the presidents are evaluated, Hayes fares as follows:

1) Making America Great
Hayes attempted, without much success, to ease the plight of the Indians in the American west, to reduce the corruption in federal

employment, and to prevent the freed blacks in the South from being disenfranchised after the end of Reconstruction. His efforts at least gave the impression that the hope of America was to be a better place.

2) Improving Quality of Life

Hayes removed federal troops from the states of the former confederacy, thereby essentially ending Reconstruction. This eliminated a major sore spot in American society although it led to several decades of second-class citizenship for former slaves and their offspring.

3) Meeting Crises

The major crisis of Hayes' administration was his acceptance of the office of president. It was fairly clear to most people that his opponent, Samuel Tilden, was entitled to victory, but the means of settling the question of disputed electoral votes guaranteed Hayes' victory. Hayes attempted to reduce the conflict between the Native Americans and settlers in the west, albeit in a one-sided fashion, by an executive order banning the sale of firearms to the Indians.

4) Overcoming Opposition

Hayes was referred to as "His Fraudulency" and other terms were used to describe him in office. He was unpopular with Republicans as well as Democrats and was lucky to accomplish what he did in his single term as it was his fate was to not be renominated for a second term.

Hayes' rating:

CATEGORY	VALUE	RATING
1) Making America Great	10	50%
2) Improving Quality of Life	8	50%
3) Meeting Crises	10	50%
4) Overcoming Opposition	8	60%

Total rating: 18.8

CHAPTER 8 – THE "AVERAGE" PRESIDENTS

The presidents in this group can be said to have not accomplished great things, but neither did their actions lead to disasters, great or small. Some have been ridiculed as "do nothing" presidents, but there have been periods in United States history when Congress took the initiative in Washington and was unwilling to give it up without a fight.

21) Benjamin Harrison, Republican

Benjamin Harrison did very little, either good or bad, during his four-year presidency, making his the definitive "nominal" or "average" presidency, almost as unexciting as his grandfather's. Benjamin Harrison believed that Congress was the true voice of the people, and the president should limit himself to following the will of Congress, at least in domestic matters.

Regarding the qualities by which the presidents are evaluated, Benjamin Harrison fares as follows:

1) Making America Great

   Harrison, with his Secretary of State, James G. Blaine, hosted the first Pan-American Congress, in Washington in 1889. He expanded the United States Navy, but also entered into international arbitration to resolve disputes with other countries. Benjamin Harrison thus anticipated Theodore Roosevelt's "walk softly but carry a big stick."

2) Improving Quality of Life
    Benjamin Harrison favored the high protective tariffs voted by Congress, that protected American industry, giving more jobs at better pay to working-class Americans but also causing higher prices; he warned that the prosperity of the American worker would suffer if the lower tariffs proposed by the Democrats, who took over the House of Representatives in the 1892 elections, were to be enacted.

3) Meeting Crises
    The Sherman Anti-Trust Act was passed during Benjamin Harrison's administration, providing the mechanism for control of the emerging huge trusts that would control American heavy industry, but successful prosecutions would await the future. Harrison strongly proposed an anti-lynching law be enacted by Congress so that he could use federal force to end racial lawlessness in the South.

4) Overcoming Opposition
    Republicans were in control of the House and Senate when Benjamin Harrison entered the presidency. The House went Democrat in the 52nd Congress and Benjamin Harrison lost his reelection bid in 1892 in a 3-man race.

Benjamin Harrison's rating:

CATEGORY	VALUE	RATING
1) Making America Great	10	50%
2) Improving Quality of Life	8	50%
3) Meeting Crises	10	50%
4) Overcoming Opposition	8	50%

Total rating: 18.0

22) James A Garfield, Republican

Garfield had almost no chance to do anything positive for the American people as President as he was assassinated not too long after taking office. This, of course, also minimizes the damage he might have been able to do, had he been so inclined. Ironically, one of his goals as president was civil-service reform; he was assassinated by a disappointed office-seeker.

Regarding the qualities by which the presidents are evaluated, Garfield fares as follows:

1) Making America Great

   With people like John D. Rockefeller and Andrew Carnegie developing their companies, the United States was on its way to world power status as Garfield entered the White House.

2) Improving Quality of Life

   As Garfield took office as president, the United States was recovering from the effects of the depression and labor strife of the 1870s. Garfield did nothing to slow down that recovery.

3) Meeting Crises

   Garfield had no opportunity to deal with any crisis that might have developed during his seven-month presidency.

4) Overcoming Opposition

   Garfield was a beneficiary of the "payoffs," if they could be called that, from the Credit Mobilier scandal. This allowed some opposition to him to arise before and during his presidency.

Garfield's rating:

CATEGORY	VALUE	RATING
1) Making America Great	10	50%
2) Improving Quality of Life	8	50%
3) Meeting Crises	10	50%
4) Overcoming Opposition	8	50%

Total rating: 18.0

23) Donald Trump, Republican

It is impossible to objectively evaluate Donald Trump in April 2020. It is impossible to observe the long-term effects of his policies, some of which have been enacted and some of which have not. He has just now been forced to deal with a major crisis. He is facing strenuous opposition, but it is not yet clear whether he will eventually overcome it.

Regarding the qualities by which the presidents are evaluated, Trump fares as follows, noting that at the time of this writing (April 30, 2020) Trump has not served all of his first term as president:

1) Making America Great
    Trump has had success in reducing the loss of high-paying skilled manufacturing jobs to overseas, and has renegotiated trade agreements with Mexico, Canada, and China to help American exports.

2) Improving Quality of Life
    The day after the 2016 election results were announced, the United States' economy began a recovery that has continued through the first half of Trump's first term. During the previous eight years, whatever economic recovery that existed was largely the result of federal government stimulus spending.

3) Meeting Crises
    The number of illegal aliens crossing the southern border between the United States and Mexico has dropped dramatically since Trump took office. The results of his response to the coronavirus crisis is yet to be determined.

4) Overcoming Opposition
    The Democratic Party took immediate steps to destroy the Trump presidency even before he took office in January 2017. The result of this fight is not yet in.

Trump's rating is purely nominal, as the permanent effects of his policies cannot be determined at this time (April 2020):

CATEGORY	VALUE	RATING
1) Making America Great	10	50%
2) Improving Quality of Life	8	50%
3) Meeting Crises	10	50%
4) Overcoming Opposition	8	50%

Total rating: 18.0

24) William Henry Harrison, Whig

William Henry Harrison was the first member of the Whig, or Anti-Andrew-Jackson, Party to win the presidency. This only occurred after the effects of Jackson's poor fiscal policies came home to roost, under Jackson's anointed successor, Martin Van Buren. Harrison received over 53% of the popular vote in the election of 1840, perhaps partly due to the Whig Party's inauguration of several seemingly modern campaign tactics, including parades, banners, songs and slogans.

William Henry Harrison was an invalid from the date of his inauguration until he died 31 days later. He thus has no record, as president, upon which to rate him as president. His inaugural address revealed his true Whig leanings; he proposed a single term for the president, and strongly condemned the "impropriety of Executive interference in the legislation of Congress." Harrison claimed that the constitutional duty of the president to communicate information to Congress, and constitutional authority to recommend measures did not give him the right to originate legislation. This continued to be Whig, and later Republican, philosophy, but suffered many exceptions.

Regarding the qualities by which the presidents are evaluated, William Henry Harrison fares as follows:

1) Making America Great

    William Henry Harrison was a key figure in the opening of the Old Northwest, now the states of Ohio, Indiana, Illinois, Michigan, and Wisconsin, to settlement by pioneers from the eastern states and Europe. That he trammeled on the rights of the Native Americans, the Indians, was not considered a serious offense by most Americans at the time.

2) Improving Quality of Life
While governor of Indiana Territory, William Henry Harrison provided an environment conducive to the welfare of the pioneer settlers, leading to admission of Indiana as a state in 1816.

3) Meeting Crises
William Henry Harrison successfully fought the Battle of Tippecanoe north of present Lafayette, Indiana, in 1811, removing the threat of Tecumseh and the Shawnees from the Midwest.

4) Overcoming Opposition
In spite of ridicule by the Democrats as being a frontier bumpkin, William Henry Harrison easily won the presidential election of 1840 over his opponent, the incumbent, Martin Van Buren. This, election as the first Whig president, while the vast majority of voters in the United States considered themselves Democrats, was Harrison's only presidential achievement.

William Henry Harrison's rating:

CATEGORY	VALUE	RATING
1) Making America Great	10	50%
2) Improving Quality of Life	8	50%
3) Meeting Crises	10	50%
4) Overcoming Opposition	8	50%

Total rating: 18.0

25) Grover Cleveland (1st Term), Democrat

Grover Cleveland was able to exploit the Republican Party's nomination of James G. Blaine, who was tainted by corruption, as their candidate in the 1884 presidential election. Cleveland won by garnering only 50.3 percent of the popular vote. Many liberal Republicans stayed home or crossed party lines and voted Democrat, probably giving the election to Cleveland.

Regarding the qualities by which the presidents are evaluated, Grover Cleveland in his first term fares as follows:

1) Making America Great
    Cleveland exemplified honest government and helped eliminate the aura of corruption of the Reconstruction era.

2) Improving Quality of Life
    Cleveland fought against high tariffs, helping to reduce the cost of living for Americans.

3) Meeting Crises
    Industrial strife reached a climax during Cleveland's first administration with such actions as the Haymarket Riot in Chicago. Cleveland saw to the creation of the Department of Labor in an effort to mitigate management-labor disputes, although it did not achieve cabinet status until much later. The Interstate Commerce Commission, the first federal regulatory agency, also began its work under Cleveland, although it was initially largely ineffective in curbing abuses by the railroads.

4) Overcoming Opposition
    Cleveland was abused by the Republicans for opposing pensions for Grand Army of the Republic veterans and by Democrats for his opposition to the free coinage of silver.

Cleveland(1)'s rating:

CATEGORY	VALUE	RATING
1) Making America Great	10	40%
2) Improving Quality of Life	8	40%
3) Meeting Crises	10	60%
4) Overcoming Opposition	8	60%

Total rating: 18.0

CHAPTER 9 — THE BELOW-AVERAGE PRESIDENTS

Real Ranking found twenty presidents to be above average, five presidents to be "average," with ratings of 18.0, and twenty presidents to be below average. Twelve presidents, those discussed in this chapter, are only slightly below average. Four are rated "poor" and four are rated "bad" to make the total twenty. Based on a different quantitative rating system discussed in Chapter 14, on a scale of zero to 100, for ten different categories for a total potential score of 1000, with only 43 presidential ratings – Trump was not rated and Cleveland was rated only once, combining his two separate terms into one, 27 presidents achieved a score of more than 500, or 50%. The median score was 557, achieved by U.S. Grant, with 21 presidents having higher ratings and 21 presidents having lower ratings. This different rating system was in fairly good agreement with the other eighteen rankings as identified by Wikipedia (see Chapter 14), so that it can be concluded that the Real Ranking is more rigorous than the mainstream. On the other hand, a libertarian ranking as promulgated by Ivan Eland (see page 29) (not included in the Wikipedia mainstream ranking composite) ranks four presidents as average, only ten as above average ("good" and "excellent") and twenty-seven as below average ("poor" and "bad"). Only one president, Dwight Eisenhower, receives a similar ranking by all three. It would thus appear that only the Real Ranking provides an even-handed picture of the presidents.

26) Grover Cleveland (2nd Term), Democrat

Grover Cleveland is the only president of the United States to have served non-consecutive terms. He was defeated for reelection by Benjamin Harrison in 1888 but then defeated Harrison in Harrison's bid for reelection in 1892. As conditions and Cleveland's public standing were different in his two terms he is listed twice here, and is officially considered the 22nd and 24th presidents by the United States government. Most presidential ratings and rankings evaluate Cleveland once, combining his two terms into one. As can be seen, there is not a great deal of difference between his two terms. Cleveland in his second term rates slightly below the average rating of all the presidents, with a rating of 17.6 as opposed to the average rating of all 45 presidents of 17.64.

Regarding the qualities by which the presidents are evaluated, Grover Cleveland in his second term fares as follows:

1) Making America Great
    Cleveland resisted the annexation of Hawaii, which was not achieved until the McKinley administration.

2) Improving Quality of Life
    Cleveland, with the help of the Republicans, was able to repeal the Sherman Silver Purchase Act, which was rapidly draining gold from the United States Treasury.

3) Meeting Crises
    Labor unrest and other factors caused a drag on the United States economy that led to depression that was not ended by the time of the 1896 election.

4) Overcoming Opposition
    Cleveland was again under attack from Democrats for his conservative policies, particularly his support of the gold standard and his opposition to the Pullman Strike and Coxey's Army of unemployed. He was replaced as the Democratic Party nominee in the 1896 presidential election by William Jennings Bryan, an outspoken populist.

Cleveland(2)'s rating:

CATEGORY	VALUE	RATING
1) Making America Great	10	40%
2) Improving Quality of Life	8	35%
3) Meeting Crises	10	60%
4) Overcoming Opposition	8	60%

Total rating: 17.6

27) George W. Bush, Republican

George Walker Bush was one of the half-dozen or so presidents whose election was so close and contentious that it affected his performance in his first term of office. At the end of the 2000 presidential election day, the outcome in several states was in doubt. The news media first declared a victory for the Democratic Party candidate, Al Gore, then reversed itself to declare Bush the victor, then backed off on that. Eventually Bush was named the victor after the United States Supreme Court got involved, particularly regarding the counting of votes in Florida, one of the undecided states. As with John Quincy Adams after the 1824 election, and Rutherford B. Hayes after the 1876 election, George W. Bush was not accepted initially as president by a large segment of the population of the country. Fortunately for Bush, he won reelection with a clear majority of the popular and electoral vote in 2004, and the complaints died down. Like Benjamin Harrison, coincidentally another victor in a contentious presidential election, George W. Bush can be considered a "nominal" or "average" president, as he had no great blunders and no great successes during his presidency. He received a 50% rating by Real Ranking in three of four categories as described in Chapter 4. He and Ulysses S. Grant rate slightly below the average rating of all the presidents, with a rating of 17.0 as opposed to the average rating of all 45 presidents of 17.64. A 50% average rating would be 18.0.

Regarding the qualities by which the presidents are evaluated, George W. Bush fares as follows:

1) Making America Great
    George W. Bush was able to make an immediate and powerful response to the horrific events of September 11, 2001. He led the United States in a strenuous effort to halt international terrorism and particularly to bring the perpetrators of the September 11, 2001, attacks on the World Trade Center, the Pentagon, and elsewhere to justice. He was instrumental in creation of the cabinet level Department of Homeland Security to help protect against terrorist attacks within the United States. In foreign policy, Bush tipped the United States toward Russia, China, India, Pakistan, and Japan while distancing from other traditional allies, upsetting world diplomacy.

2) Improving Quality of Life
    George W. Bush took preemptive steps to avoid a recession that appeared to be looming at the end of the Clinton Administration. George W. Bush began an education initiative to try to end substandard public school education in the United States. His "No Child Left Behind" initiative reversed traditional Republican Party lack of support for education direction at the national level.

3) Meeting Crises
    George W. Bush led an international coalition, that went on the offense against the perpetrators of the September 11 and other terrorist acts, that drove Osama bin Laden and his Al Qaeda group into hiding. He made a strong effort to convert Iraq from a dictatorship to democracy. Unfortunately, his removal of Saddam Hussein from power in Iraq resulted in further destabilization in the Middle East. The intelligence that was used to justify invasion of Iraq was later shown to be faulty. The Bush Administration led a successful international campaign to combat AIDS, improving treatment and substantially reducing the HIV infection rate. Under Bush, the federal government was forced to react to a major financial crisis when many large institutions in the United States and elsewhere began to fail in September 2008.

4) Overcoming Opposition
George W. Bush successfully overcame partisan opposition to his election in 2000, but lost the House of Representatives and the Senate to the Democrats in the 110th Congress.

George Walker Bush's rating:

CATEGORY	VALUE	RATING
1) Making America Great	10	50%
2) Improving Quality of Life	8	50%
3) Meeting Crises	10	40%
4) Overcoming Opposition	8	50%

Total rating: 17.0

28) U. S. Grant, Republican

Ulysses Simpson Grant was the great hero of the American Civil War. His leadership placed the Union armies on the path of victory and led to a successful conclusion of the military phase of the southern rebellion. Earlier, Grant participated in the Mexican War as a junior officer, and came away with a negative feeling about the war, believing it to be an unjustified conflict - which it was. He and George W. Bush rate slightly below the average rating of all the presidents, with a rating of 17.0 as opposed to the average rating of all 45 presidents of 17.64.

Regarding the qualities by which the presidents are evaluated, Grant fares as follows:

1) Making America Great
Grant achieved a measure of success in foreign relations with his appointment of Hamilton Fish as Secretary of State.

2) Improving Quality of Life
Grant supported Congress in its harsh Reconstruction policy against the South. He proposed the annexation of Santo Domingo as a haven for the freed slaves, but Congress rejected this plan.

3) Meeting Crises

Corruption among some of Grant's appointees in the federal government led to several scandals, such as the Whiskey Ring - particularly ironic since he tended to display the symptoms of alcoholism whenever he was forced by his duties, particularly in the Army, to be apart from his wife, Julia, for protracted periods of time. The scandals of his administration were resolved with no indication of personal involvement by Grant.

4) Overcoming Opposition

Opposition to what was perceived as Grant's weakness as president led to significant opposition to his reelection, but he easily defeated the candidate of the Democrats and the Liberal Republicans, Horace Greeley, in the presidential election of 1872. Grant was seriously considered for a third term disconnected from his first two, in the election of 1880, but various factors, including his health and the opposition of the liberals, kept it from happening.

Grant's rating:

CATEGORY	VALUE	RATING
1) Making America Great	10	50%
2) Improving Quality of Life	8	50%
3) Meeting Crises	10	40%
4) Overcoming Opposition	8	50%

Total rating: 17.0

29) Warren Harding, Republican

Warren Gamaliel Harding won the presidential election of 1920 with one of the highest percentages of the popular vote ever recorded, 63.8%. This was largely due to the public's strong aversion to the aftermath of World War I and the last few months of the Wilson Administration. It was more a vote *against* Wilson and the Democrats than a vote *for* Harding. Harding took his presidential responsibilities seriously, vetoing a generous veterans' bonus bill that did not provide for obtaining the funds to pay the bonus.

Regarding the qualities by which the presidents are evaluated, Harding fares as follows:

1) Making America Great

   In spite of personal lack of presidential timbre, Harding created a highly respected cabinet that took a leading role in world politics after World War I, in spite of the refusal of the United States to join the League of Nations. Harding hosted the Washington Conference for the Limitation of Armaments, which slowed down the growth of armaments.

2) Improving Quality of Life

   Harding initiated the idea of a national budget, thereby putting some order in federal spending and helping control the growth of the federal government. Harding's pressure on the big steel companies eventually resulted in a shorter working day for steelworkers.

3) Meeting Crises

   The big crisis of the Harding administration came after his death, when the Teapot Dome and other scandals came to light, none of which involved any actual wrongdoing by Harding, but exemplifying his failure to control his colleagues, and poor judgment in the selection of subordinates.

4) Overcoming Opposition

   Harding really had no opposition during his presidency. Congress remained solidly Republican throughout his tenure in the White House.

Harding's rating:

CATEGORY	VALUE	RATING
1) Making America Great	10	60%
2) Improving Quality of Life	8	60%
3) Meeting Crises	10	20%
4) Overcoming Opposition	8	50%

Total rating: 16.8

30) Millard Fillmore, Whig

Millard Fillmore, the second "president by accident," accomplished little to further Zachary Taylor's agenda; people still had little use for an un-elected president. He did fulfill one Whig aim, providing the first land grants for railroad construction. Fillmore later ran for president under the American Party (otherwise known as "Know-Nothings"), a third-party banner, but lost, coming in 3rd behind the Democrat and Republican candidates in 1856. He was one of the first third-party candidates to "throw" an election, as he probably took more votes away from John C. Fremont, the Republican candidate in 1856, than from James Buchanan, the Democratic Party candidate, giving Buchanan the victory. Fremont and Fillmore, who were substantially in agreement on most issues, combined for approximately 54 percent of the popular vote in 1856. By 1856, the Republican Party had been sufficiently established so that if the Republican candidate for president, John C. Fremont, had won, secession might have been avoided as the government in Washington would have been firmly in the hands of its friends and the southern slave power would not have had the advantages it had in 1860-61, advantages that some believe were due to treasonous activities on the part of the president, James Buchanan.

Regarding the qualities by which the presidents are evaluated, Fillmore fares as follows:

1) Making America Great
   Fillmore approved the Compromise of 1850, which did little to improve the prestige of the United States abroad.

2) Improving Quality of Life
   The Compromise of 1850 was actually a concession to the slaveholding south, doing little to improve the living conditions of Americans elsewhere, and including the Fugitive Slave Act, which made life more unpleasant for African Americans, whether slave or free. It did ease the tensions between North and South, somewhat.

3) Meeting Crises
   Fillmore's approval of the Compromise of 1850 made the slave vs.

free conflict worse, as the slaveholders felt it was not enough to satisfy them, and Free Soilers considered it an abject surrender to slavery.

4) Overcoming Opposition
Fillmore was quite unpopular by the end of his presidency, and was not given the nomination as the Whig candidate for president in 1852.

Fillmore's rating:

CATEGORY	VALUE	RATING
1) Making America Great	10	50%
2) Improving Quality of Life	8	50%
3) Meeting Crises	10	45%
4) Overcoming Opposition	8	40%

Total rating: 16.7

31) Andrew Johnson, Democrat

There is no question that Andrew Johnson had the worst time of any president, having been elected in 1864 to be Abraham Lincoln's vice president, as a Democrat, solely to form a "fusion" party (called the Union ticket) in the summer of 1864 when things were not going well for the country. He failed miserably in meeting the situation following Lincoln's assassination, but the fact that he survived impeachment against overwhelming odds when just being a Democrat was tantamount to treason in many people's eyes says something.

Regarding the qualities by which the presidents are evaluated, Andrew Johnson fares as follows:

1) Making America Great
Andrew Johnson attempted without success to implement Abraham Lincoln's method of returning the former Confederate states to the Union.

2) Improving Quality of Life
Andrew Johnson attempted without success to find a practical means to provide employment in the South for the freed slaves. Johnson

failed to implement a program, favored by some Radical Reconstructionists, of redistributing confiscated or abandoned former plantation land to freed slaves.

3) Meeting Crises

Upon the assassination of Abraham Lincoln, the first overt assassination of an American president, Andrew Johnson took over the Executive Branch of the federal government, but was unable to control many of his subordinates, including a few cabinet members, and was forced to accept the Tenure of Office Act, passed over his veto.

4) Overcoming Opposition

Andrew Johnson successfully survived impeachment by the radical majority in Congress.

Andrew Johnson's rating:

CATEGORY	VALUE	RATING
1) Making America Great	10	50%
2) Improving Quality of Life	8	50%
3) Meeting Crises	10	10%
4) Overcoming Opposition	8	75%

Total rating: 16.0

32) John Tyler, Whig to Democrat

John Tyler, once a Democrat but a foe of Andrew Jackson, ran as vice presidential candidate with William Henry Harrison's Whig Party presidential candidacy. His true leanings were suspect by the Whig party faithful, and as soon as he became president he showed his true colors by reverting to Democratic Party politics. Not trusted by either the Whigs or Democrats, he accomplished little in office, becoming a man without a party. After William Henry Harrison's death, there was some doubt as to whether Tyler, the first vice president to succeed to the office of president on the death of a president, could be considered more than an acting president;

an attempt was made to make him the first president to be impeached, but it failed. Tyler was the first president to have a veto overridden by Congress. He did advocate admission of Texas as a slave state, helping to provide a slavocracy majority in the Senate although Texas was not admitted until Tyler's term was over. Thanks to Daniel Webster, his Secretary of State, Tyler's administration saw resolution of the Maine-Canada boundary and a trade treaty with China.

Regarding the qualities by which the presidents are evaluated, Tyler fares as follows:

1) Making America Great

   Tyler was a champion of expansion, particularly in the southwest where he thought that slavery had a chance of success. Some international success occurred in the State Department while it was held by Daniel Webster, selected by William Henry Harrison. Webster resigned, however, after the work he had started under William Henry Harrison was completed. This included the Webster-Ashburton Treaty settling a United States – Canada border dispute, and the trade treaty with China.

2) Improving Quality of Life

   Tyler continued the Democratic Party policy of opposition to public improvements.

3) Meeting Crises

   Tyler strongly favored the annexation of Texas, which led to the Mexican War under his successor, James K. Polk.

4) Overcoming Opposition

   Tyler was the first president in history to have a veto overridden, on his last day in office, March 3, 1845.

Tyler's rating:

CATEGORY	VALUE	RATING
1) Making America Great	10	40%
2) Improving Quality of Life	8	45%
3) Meeting Crises	10	40%
4) Overcoming Opposition	8	40%

Total rating: 14.8

33) Martin Van Buren, Democrat

Even Democrats and liberal journalists think of Martin Van Buren as a poor president, but the outcome of his presidency wasn't all his fault. Van Buren had the unfortunate luck to become president just as Andrew Jackson's financial chickens came home to roost, resulting in the worst economic depression the country had yet seen, the worst ever except perhaps for the Great Depression of the 1930s. This was to some extent karma, as Van Buren, the "Wizard of Kinderhook" was in some ways the brains of the Jackson presidency, and his New York cronies had a hand in the fiscal finaglings that led to the almost complete collapse of the economy when Jackson won his bank war. As Jackson's vice president, Van Buren could have become president earlier if the 1835 assassination attempt on Jackson had succeeded.

During Van Buren's presidency, a U. S. Navy expedition discovered the continent of Antarctica, and U. S. warships interfered with American ships active in the African slave trade.

Regarding the qualities by which the presidents are evaluated, Van Buren fares as follows:

1) Making America Great

In attempting to correct the errors of the Jackson administration, mostly orchestrated by Van Buren and his cronies, Van Buren proposed an independent treasury system to take the revenues of the United States government out of private banks. Internationally, Van Buren sent a naval expedition around the world but accepted arbitration in most of the disputes between the United States and other countries.

2) Improving Quality of Life
   Van Buren declared it was not the province of the federal government
   to alleviate the sufferings of its citizens when financial panic turned
   to depression shortly after he was inaugurated.

3) Meeting Crises
   Van Buren managed to avoid full-scale war when boundary disputes
   with Britain over the Canadian-Maine border erupted.

4) Overcoming Opposition
   Van Buren faced little opposition until the end of his term. Then, as
   the Whigs chanted, "Van, Van, is a used-up man", Van Buren lost the
   1840 election in a landslide.

Van Buren's rating:

CATEGORY	VALUE	RATING
1) Making America Great	10	40%
2) Improving Quality of Life	8	35%
3) Meeting Crises	10	40%
4) Overcoming Opposition	8	40%

Total rating: 14.0

34) Jimmy Carter, Democrat

Carter ran for president on a policy of economy in government based on his
"zero" budgeting techniques he used as governor of Georgia. He also stressed
his Naval experience with nuclear reactors as qualifying him on energy issues
(the United States was still suffering from the Arab oil boycott). Carter accomplished little in Washington as his outsider status gave him little comfort
in his battles with the Washington professionals.

Regarding the qualities by which the presidents are evaluated, Carter fares
as follows:

1) Making America Great
   Jimmy Carter hosted a summit conference between Menachem Begin

of Israel and Anwar Sadat of Egypt that was hoped to be a prelude to the end of hostilities in the Middle East. These hopes were eventually thwarted as the other Arab nations looked upon Sadat, who was eventually assassinated, as a traitor to the Arab cause. Carter first cut defense spending and then increased it, adding to the unsureness with which foreign governments viewed the United States. Fidel Castro in 1980 duped Carter into accepting approximately 125,000 Cuban "refugees" who were actually undesirables, including criminals, whom Castro was happy to be rid of, in what was called the Mariel Boatlift. In 1977, Carter signed a treaty turning over the Panama Canal and the Canal Zone to the country of Panama in 1999. Carter negotiated a new Strategic Arms Limitation Treaty (SALT II) with the Soviet Union, but had to forgo ratification as the Soviets invaded Afghanistan in December of 1979, shortly after agreeing on the treaty. Carter took several punitive steps against the Soviets in retaliation, including a grain embargo and a boycott of the 1980 Moscow Summer Olympics. Carter won the Nobel Peace Prize in 2002.

2) Improving Quality of Life

Domestically, Carter's presidency can be summed up by a phrase uttered publicly by his victorious opponent in the 1980 presidential election, Ronald Reagan: "Are you better off than you were four years ago?" The answer was "NO." Carter's popularity suffered in 1980 due to a severe recession that peaked that year. Carter gave full amnesty to all Viet Nam era draft resisters. Inflation grew to unprecedented heights while Carter was president, negating the intended beneficial economic effects of tax cuts enacted during his administration. The federal Department of Energy and Department of Education were created during Carter's presidency.

3) Meeting Crises

In spite of strenuous efforts, Carter was unable to resolve the Iran Hostage Crisis, which arose after Carter allowed the Shah, who had been in exile, to come to the United States for medical treatment.

4) Overcoming Opposition

It was a foregone conclusion that Carter could not win the 1980 election, but he insisted on holding on to his delegates at the Democratic National Convention. He lost the general election with barely 41 percent of the vote to Ronald Reagan, the Republican nominee, 35,481,435 to Reagan's 43,899,248 while liberal Republican John Anderson received 5,719,437. Carter won 49 electoral votes to Reagan's 489. Carter was one of the few presidents to have his vetoes overridden when Congress was controlled by his own party.

Carter's rating:

CATEGORY	VALUE	RATING
1) Making America Great	10	40%
2) Improving Quality of Life	8	35%
3) Meeting Crises	10	35%
4) Overcoming Opposition	8	45%

Total rating: 13.9

35) Franklin D. Roosevelt, Democrat

Franklin Delano Roosevelt, throughout his presidency, was probably the most popular of presidents, although his winning margins in the Electoral College and the popular vote eventually declined significantly. Unfortunately, he failed at his main missions. His policies did not end the Great Depression in the United States, and are considered by some to have prolonged it. He also failed to end totalitarianism, in Europe or in Asia. The Soviet Union, with no real opposition from the United States, took over from Nazi Germany as the oppressor of Eastern Europe, and China with Russian assistance replaced Japan as the dominant force in East Asia.

Franklin Delano Roosevelt is credited with inspiring the people of the United States with confidence in the United States government and faith in democracy, at a time when many, including Charles Lindbergh and Joseph P. Kennedy, seemed to think that fascism was the wave of the future. The first of Roosevelt's famous "fireside chats" explained why he closed the nation's banks.

Franklin Delano Roosevelt's exemplary political skills propelled him to the peak of presidential power, after his initial success in 1932 was practically guaranteed as the vast majority of the people of the United States were desperate for a change in administration in Washington as the economic depression deepened under the presidency of Herbert Hoover, the last Republican in a nearly unbroken series going back to Abraham Lincoln's victory of 1860. Roosevelt's innovative use of radio as a means of communicating directly with the public contrasts sharply with his secret machinations to maintain the Democratic Party in power in Washington. After Roosevelt's economic policies failed to end the depression, Roosevelt lost interest in domestic politics as the international situation darkened. He was unable to interest the country in an active international antifascist role, but was extremely active, up to the limit of his executive powers, in supporting the United Kingdom in its war against Nazi Germany. Unfortunately, Roosevelt failed disastrously in several areas prior to and during World War II.

Even before the United States entered the war, German submarines were successfully destroying shipping in the North Atlantic. Supposedly in order to prevent panic among the American populace, but more likely to avoid culpability and loss of confidence in his administration, Roosevelt ordered the sinking of merchant shipping off the east coast of the United States to be kept secret, and failed to take any measures to reduce the damage. This led to much greater losses, that could have been avoided.

The failure of the United States military forces to protect the U.S. Navy fleet at Pearl Harbor is considered a major failing, and several high level officers were court-martialed over it. The truth is that United States and British intelligence forces had broken the Japanese codes, but failed to provide adequate warning to the forces in Hawaii.

In Europe, Roosevelt gave in to British demands for retribution against the Germans for their attacks on English cities, particularly London. Thousands of bombers and crews were lost in so-called "strategic" bombing that killed hundreds of thousands of German, French, and other civilians while doing little to slow the German war effort. If these air attacks had been directed to tactical use against the German Army, it is likely that war in Europe could have been significantly shortened. It would also have resulted in much less devastation across Europe after the war and recovery could have occurred sooner. It might also have resulted in the "Iron Curtain" having been erected hundreds of miles further east, easing Cold War pressures.

Regarding the qualities by which the presidents are evaluated, Franklin Delano Roosevelt fares as follows:

1) Making America Great

   Franklin Roosevelt attempted to do as much as possible to thwart the fascist totalitarian governments of Germany, Italy, and Japan from expanding, but was almost completely stymied by the isolationism of the United States Congress. He did get some revision of the neutrality rules out of Congress and was able to provide some aid to Great Britain and her allies. He prepared, with Winston Churchill, the Atlantic Charter in August of 1941, spelling out war aims against Germany and Japan. When the United States entered World War II, Roosevelt immediately put the entire strength of the nation to work to defeat Hitler and Japan. But his errors in Hawaii and Europe prolonged the war and increased its devastation. Unfortunately, he allowed Joseph Stalin, dictator of the Soviet Union, to completely overrun eastern Europe, resulting in the enslavement of those very eastern European persons who the United States, France, and Great Britain went to war in Europe to protect. Roosevelt's diplomatic recognition of the Soviet Union encouraged Stalin in his repressive and expansionist activities. The liberation of France did little to improve the international status of the United States, as France later, under the very Charles De Gaulle who Roosevelt helped put in power in France, took an independent, almost anti-United States stance in post-World War II politics. Roosevelt's strategic failures against Japan resulted in the necessity of dropping atomic bombs to force Japan into surrender. In Asia, it was the Chinese who emerged as the greater threat after the Japanese were defeated.

2) Improving Quality of Life

   Franklin Roosevelt was elected in 1932 in opposition to what was considered Herbert Hoover's lackluster efforts to end the depression that began in 1929. In spite of massive increases in government expenditure, and gross increases in federal government controls over society, by such measures as the Agricultural Adjustment Act, the National Industrial Recovery Act, the Tennessee Valley Authority, the Federal Communications Commission, the Federal Housing Administration, the National Resources Board, the Rural Electrification Administration, and the Home Owners Loan Corporation, the depression was not ended; there is some reason to believe that government intervention in the economy thwarted a recovery that had begun in 1937 and put the economy back in recession in 1938. Roosevelt by executive order took the country off the gold standard, in spite of this, by the Constitution, being clearly the responsibility of Congress. The depression did not end until the country went on a full war economy in 1942. All these activities greatly increased the power of the National government over the states, in a body blow to federalism, obtained by bribery methods such as the Federal Emergency Relief Administration, Social Security, and the Civilian Conservation Corps, relieving the state and local governments of the expense of providing direct relief to the destitute, young, old, and working-class.

When the United States entered World War II, Roosevelt obtained rigid price and wage controls, hundreds of billions of dollars in appropriations, censorship, a ban on strikes and lockouts, and secret development of the atomic bomb.

3) Meeting Crises

The first crisis faced by Franklin Delano Roosevelt was the Great Depression. While it did not have the deleterious effect on the United States as did the depression of 1837, it did have a severe negative impact on a great many Americans. Franklin Roosevelt's major accomplishment in combatting the Great Depression was to act as cheerleader to convince the American people that good times would eventually return. Roosevelt attempted to increase the number of Supreme Court Justices to tilt the court toward approval of his New Deal measures. This move was looked at as "packing" the court and was defeated. As it turned out, Roosevelt, over his twelve years as president, appointed nine Supreme Court justices anyway. When choosing a running mate for the 1944 presidential election, in the midst of World War II, Roosevelt, in spite of his poor and worsening health (many think he should have never run, in 1944 or 1940), picked Harry Truman, a relatively unknown, unsophisticated United States Senator from Missouri as his running mate, and then ignored him and left him out of policy discussions and important briefings.

4)   Overcoming Opposition
Franklin Delano Roosevelt won 59.1 percent of the popular vote in 1932, 62.5 percent in 1936, 55 percent in 1940, and 53.8 percent in 1944. After his triumphant reelection in 1936, his popularity dwindled as many people felt he had served long enough.

Franklin Delano Roosevelt's rating:

CATEGORY	VALUE	RATING
1) Making America Great	10	30%
2) Improving Quality of Life	8	30%
3) Meeting Crises	10	45%
4) Overcoming Opposition	8	45%

Total rating: 13.5

36) Harry Truman, Democrat

Truman inherited the presidency from Franklin Delano Roosevelt, but in spite of Roosevelt's extremely poor health no effort was made to prepare Truman for the job. Truman had to end both the war in Europe and the war in Asia, and had to keep both the real "victors" of the war, Russia and China, at bay. He did not do well at either task, but he might have performed better if given the proper training prior to taking his job. Truman largely continued the policies and programs of Franklin Roosevelt, with many of the same staff and Cabinet members as those who served under Roosevelt.

Regarding the qualities by which the presidents are evaluated, Truman fares as follows:

1) Making America Great

   Truman ordered the dropping of atomic bombs on Japan, essentially ending World War II, but an act that remains controversial to this day. Truman was slow to recognize the expansionist aims of Joseph Stalin, head of the Soviet Union, after the end of World War II in Europe. Truman ended up bogged down in a land war in Korea after the Russians and Communist Chinese urged the North Koreans to invade the south in 1950. Truman fired General Douglas MacArthur, head of U.S. and other United Nations troops in Korea, rather than accede to his requests to fight all-out against the Communists. Truman enunciated the "Truman Doctrine" as a counter to Communism, specifically to prevent outside forces, particularly Soviet Russia, from interfering in the domestic policies of sovereign nations. Truman applied his doctrine to Greece, where the communist threat was relatively weak and largely domestic, in a successful endeavor, while allowing Czechoslovakia, Romania, Bulgaria, Hungary, Poland, and East Germany to become Russian Soviet satellites without any effort or offers of aid above the Marshall Plan, the aid of which each of these countries refused on orders from Moscow. Truman's administration propounded the "Containment" policy, intended to restrict the expansion of Communism, with poor results. Truman signed the treaty forming the North Atlantic Treaty Organization in 1949, in response to Communist encroachments including the blockading of Berlin, Germany. Truman immediately recognized the state of Israel on its creation in 1948 instantly winning the enmity of the entire Arab world.

2) Improving Quality of Life

   Truman enacted strong controls on the economy after World War II ended, in a futile attempt to control inflation. He seized United States steel mills in an effort to prevent strikes, but was overruled by the Supreme Court.

3) Meeting Crises

   Truman failed to prevent the takeover of the Chinese mainland by Mao Tse Tung's communists.

4) Overcoming Opposition

Truman was unable to enact most of his proposals as president due to opposition by a combination of Republicans and Southern Democrats. He chose not to run for reelection in 1952, although he was constitutionally allowed to do so.

Truman's rating:

CATEGORY	VALUE	RATING
1) Making America Great	10	40%
2) Improving Quality of Life	8	25%
3) Meeting Crises	10	35%
4) Overcoming Opposition	8	45%

Total rating: 13.1

37) William J. Clinton, Democrat

Clinton entered the presidency with a Democrat-controlled Congress and a strong agenda for social programs including additional child welfare programs and expanded Medicare. When the cost and scope of these proposed programs were fully explained to the public, Clinton's entire liberal program was rejected out of hand, as both the House of Representatives and the Senate turned Republican in the 104th Congress elected in 1994 and remained so throughout Clinton's presidency. Clinton accepted the defeat of his Democrat Congress, and went so far as to accept a balanced budget and no annual federal deficit by the end of his administration, the first time the federal budget had balanced since 1969.

Several scandals erupted during Clinton's presidency, some relating to his career as governor in Arkansas, such as the Whitewater land deal affair and the Rose law firm, and others of a personal nature, including activities involving a White House intern and the suicide of Vincent Foster, an aide to President Clinton. In a case that went to the United States Supreme Court, a former employee of the State of Arkansas, Paula Jones, accused Clinton of sexual harassment.

Regarding the qualities by which the presidents are evaluated, Clinton fares as follows:

1) Making America Great
   After the end of the Soviet Union, engineered by the previous administration, Clinton squandered the "peace dividend" and allowed the
   armed forces of the United States to deteriorate. An attempt at using
   United States combat troops to provide humanitarian aid in Somalia
   failed disastrously. Clinton was able to broker a deal between Yasir
   Arafat and Israeli Prime Minister Benjamin Netanyahu, but it did not
   lead to long-term gains. On December 15, 1998, Clinton ordered the
   American military to attack targets in Iraq after reports surfaced of
   hidden weapons of mass destruction.

2) Improving Quality of Life
   Clinton's pressure on banks to increase their lending to people at the
   lower end of the economic ladder eventually, with other Administration actions, resulted in massive foreclosures and aggravated the crisis
   in the banking industry in the United States. Clinton attempted but
   failed to get health care reform legislation enacted. Clinton signed
   agreements enacting expanded North American and world-wide trade
   as a culmination of efforts begun under his predecessor, George Herbert Walker Bush.

3) Meeting Crises
   Clinton's handling of a Bureau of Alcohol, Tobacco, and Firearms
   (ATF) incident in Waco, Texas, resulted in the deaths of eighty or
   more people, including seventeen children. The Oklahoma City
   bombing was a direct domestic terrorist response to this.

4) Overcoming Opposition
   Clinton successfully overcame impeachment by the House of Representatives, even though 31 members of his own Democratic Party in
   the House of Representatives voted with the Republican majority for
   impeachment. Two votes were held in his trial in the Senate. He won
   the first, 55 to only 44 for removal from office, and won the second
   by a 50-50 tie vote. A two-thirds majority, 67 votes, was required for
   conviction. Before the end of his second term, Clinton had largely

abrogated his leadership position and turned the initiative in Washington over to the Republican-controlled Congress. This resulted in enaction of balanced-budget legislation, tax cuts, and limiting increases in Medicare.

Clinton's Rating:

CATEGORY	VALUE	RATING
1) Making America Great	10	30%
2) Improving Quality of Life	8	30%
3) Meeting Crises	10	25%
4) Overcoming Opposition	8	50%

Total rating: 11.9

CHAPTER 10 – THE POOR PRESIDENTS

Several presidents entered office with high hopes, and public support, but were not up to the challenge, perhaps facing greater, more difficult tasks than they expected. And as Harry Truman said about his presidential desk, "The buck stops here."

38) John F. Kennedy, Democrat

John F. Kennedy was considered by many, including the Russians, as a political lightweight, owing his election to the presidency more to his father's millions than to any innate leadership, diplomatic, or political qualities he might have had. There is considerable suspicion that Joseph P. Kennedy, John F.'s father, paid for some dirty tricks in West Virginia and perhaps elsewhere to get his son the Democratic Party presidential nomination over the leading contender, Hubert Humphrey of Minnesota, and that the Kennedys may have assisted Richard J. Daley, the Irish-American mayor of Chicago, in manufacturing votes to get Kennedy the win in the 1960 presidential election over Richard Nixon of California. Kennedy appeared to have toughened up after taking some particularly hard knocks early in his presidency, but was assassinated before he was able to make more mistakes or profit from his experiences.

Kennedy was perhaps the first real "public relations" president, with a great deal of effort being expended before, during, and after his presidency to keep his image polished.

Regarding the qualities by which the presidents are evaluated, Kennedy fares as follows:

1) Making America Great

After the failure of the Bay of Pigs invasion, the Soviets decided that Kennedy was a weak president and that the Soviets could make advances in many areas. One of the first was in Berlin, where a wall was built surrounding West Berlin, greatly reducing the number of persons escaping East Germany by crossing over into West Berlin. Several other Soviet moves prompted the Kennedy administration to make a forceful move against the advance of communism. It was decided to mount a military campaign in Viet Nam, to assist the South Vietnamese in repulsing communist infiltration. This move eventually failed, and cost much in United States prestige abroad as it progressed. No one knows how many state secrets may have been revealed to the opposition via Kennedy's supposedly frequent liaisons with women of questionable virtue. Kennedy was instrumental in forming the Peace Corps, which turned out to be more an effective way of providing upper-middle-class American children a post-college-graduation overseas vacation with pay than a tool for improving United States foreign relations. After agreeing to a halt in nuclear weapons testing during the Eisenhower administration, the Russians began again to detonate nuclear bombs shortly after the Kennedy administration began in 1961. A Nuclear Test Ban treaty was eventually signed in 1963. The United States space program was actively accelerated during the Kennedy administration, eventually resulting, in 1969, in the first landing on the Moon.

2) Improving Quality of Life

Kennedy was unable to get Congressional approval for his many proposed domestic programs for a wide variety of purposes. He was instrumental, while a Senator, in defeating a proposed Constitutional Amendment that would have divided up each state's electoral vote according to percentage of popular vote – a proposal favored at that time by conservatives, but later by liberals as an approach to having the popular vote decide the winner of presidential elections. The minimum wage was raised to $1.25 per hour during the Kennedy administration. Kennedy actively engaged in promoting improved civil rights for black Americans, particularly in Alabama and Mississippi.

3) Meeting Crises

John F. Kennedy faced many crises in his short tenure as president. His response to each was not good. He basically ignored the Bay of Pigs invasion, resulting in severe animosity from the participants and supporters of that exercise, which was sponsored by the United States government. Kennedy responded more vigorously to the Russian installation of offensive missiles in Cuba, but he allowed a "win" on the part of the Russians by trading removal of NATO missiles from Turkey in exchange for withdrawal of the Russian missiles from Cuba. Kennedy's response to the erection of the Berlin Wall, a major slap by the Russians, was to begin the massive buildup of United States troops in Viet Nam, a major error.

4) Overcoming Opposition

Despite his great personal popularity, Kennedy was unable to obtain much in the way of liberal social legislation from Congress, and faced reduced prestige abroad as the Soviets continued to score victories in many areas, in spite of increased U.S. defense spending.

Kennedy's rating:

CATEGORY	VALUE	RATING
1) Making America Great	10	30%
2) Improving Quality of Life	8	40%
3) Meeting Crises	10	10%
4) Overcoming Opposition	8	35%

Total rating: 10.0

39) James Madison, "Republican"*

James Madison was one of the leading figures in the development and adoption of the United States Constitution, but he became a states' rights advocate after the Constitution was adopted and Alexander Hamilton, as Washington's Secretary of the Treasury, molded government policy to favor the financial interests of the country. He was considered to be one of the political geniuses behind Thomas Jefferson's development of the "Republican" (later Democratic) party on the basis of Anti-federalism. This would be the beginning of the southern "states rights" strategy.

Regarding the qualities by which the presidents are evaluated, Madison fares as follows:

1) Making America Great
   Madison was goaded into declaring war on Great Britain but was lucky to get a peace treaty ending the war that returned things to their antebellum status.

2) Improving Quality of Life
   British victories in the War of 1812 encouraged Indians who mounted increased campaigns of massacres along the frontiers until defeated by Andrew Jackson and William Henry Harrison.

3) Meeting Crises
   Madison was forced to abandon Washington when the British attacked and set fire to the Capitol, the White House, and other buildings.

4) Overcoming Opposition
   Madison, like Bill Clinton almost 200 years later, followed an "if you can't beat them, join them" strategy after his popularity plummeted. He reversed his opposition to a national bank and signed legislation for a new bank. He also called for higher tariffs, another Federalist pet project. He did, however, just before leaving office at the end of his second term, veto the Bonus Bill that would have used federal funds to build "a perfect system of roads…" as proposed by John C. Calhoun.

---

*The party of Thomas Jefferson, not the party of Abraham Lincoln.

Madison's rating:

CATEGORY	VALUE	RATING
1) Making America Great	10	25%
2) Improving Quality of Life	8	40%
3) Meeting Crises	10	10%
4) Overcoming Opposition	8	40%

Total rating: 9.9

40) Woodrow Wilson, Democrat

Woodrow Wilson had a brief political career, having been only governor of New Jersey for a single term before being elected president. This was more a help than a hindrance to him, as he had no political baggage as compared to his rivals for the Democratic Party nomination for president in 1912. Wilson was also an avowed progressive, although of the lily-white southern variety (most of his life had been spent south of the Mason-Dixon Line before becoming president of Princeton University). His progressivism made him attractive as a possible magnet for dissatisfied Republican progressive voters.

Wilson as president received credit for progressive programs actually initiated by his Republican predecessor, William Howard Taft, including the income tax and direct election of senators.

Regarding the qualities by which the presidents are evaluated, Wilson fares as follows:

1) Making America Great

Woodrow Wilson pushed the United States into World War I, after early attempts to avoid entry into the conflict. His efforts at the peace conference gave away the conditions of the peace to Great Britain and France, in return for their agreeing to foundation of a League of Nations, Wilson's pet project that the United States eventually refused to join. The harsh peace terms forced onto the Central Powers, Germany and Austria, by the Allies after Wilson gave them a free hand led directly to the Great Depression of the 1930s and World War II. An argument can also be made that the policies of Wilson, Britain, and France allowed the success of the communist revolution in Russia, the effects of which lasted for 70 years, if, in fact, they are concluded now. Wilson's heavy-handed expansion of United States intervention-ism in Latin America resulted in resentment of the United States by the people of those countries that lasted for decades.

2) Improving Quality of Life

Wilson orchestrated the passing of highly restrictive laws that practically turned the United States into a police state, in supposed advancement of prosecution of the Great War (World War I). Wilson's progressive economic policies were frankly socialist in regard to the nation's rail-roads, caving to the demands of labor unions for government control of the railroads, which amounted to confiscation with inadequate compen-sation, and left them a shambles after government control ended.

Wilson obtained reduction in tariffs after he was elected pres-ident, but the advent of World War I shortly after meant that fewer foreign goods were available for import into the United States. Wil-son and the Democrat-controlled Congress did accomplish consid-erable consumer-friendly legislation, including creating the Federal Trade Commission, the Clayton anti-trust act, and child labor legis-lation. Wilson also pushed adoption of the Adamson Act, benefitting railroad employees.

3) Meeting Crises

Wilson continually ignored serious challenges to the sovereignty of the United States by agents of the central powers, and torpedoing of American vessels by German submarines. Wilson did not see fit to ask for a declaration of war until Congress passed the Adamson Act, a pro-labor measure that also gave the president vigorous powers to act on the domestic economy of the United States. After obtaining Democratic Party control of Congress with his anti-war rhetoric, Wilson proceeded to demand, and receive, a declaration of war from Congress, and obtained what was tantamount to dictatorial powers throughout American participation in the conflict. As noted above, his obsession with the League of Nation squandered his leadership position as the de facto head of the Allied Powers at the time of the

Armistice, resulting in devastation and chaos in Europe that lasted, essentially, until the 1950s.

4) Overcoming Opposition

After Wilson was unable to get approval from the United States Senate of the Versailles Treaty including the League of Nations, he went on a nationwide speaking tour trying to build public support for the treaty. He failed to move public opinion, and succumbed to a stroke and had to return to Washington, completely debilitated. In spite of his condition, he refused to give up executive power, but acted through his wife. This led to the complete abandonment of Wilson and Wilsonianism by the public and the politicians.

Wilson's rating:

CATEGORY		VALUE	RATING
1)	Making America Great	10	25%
2)	Improving Quality of Life	8	25%
3)	Meeting Crises	10	40%
4)	Overcoming Opposition	8	15%

Total rating: 9.7

41) Barrack Obama, Democrat

After a brief career as an elected politician, Obama captured the enthusiasm of liberals throughout the country and defeated Hillary Clinton for the Democratic Party nomination for president of the United States in 2008.

Not unlike Bill Clinton before him, Barrack Obama entered the Oval Office with what he considered a mandate for liberal change, and had a Democrat Congress to support him. Also not unlike Clinton, Obama discovered that the public was not as fond of his liberal agenda as he initially believed. The next House of Representatives, in the 112th Congress, went Republican, and the House stayed that way throughout the Obama presidency. The Senate eventually followed suit, turning Republican in the 114th Congress in 2014 and remaining so to the present day (April 2020).

Regarding the qualities by which the presidents are evaluated, Obama fares as follows:

1) Making America Great
    Obama's major accomplishment in foreign affairs was the execution of Osama bin Laden, long after he had become a hunted fugitive irrelevant in international affairs. This was a political assassination, contrary to the rule of law, and in stark contrast to the arrest, trial, and execution of Saddam Hussein in Iraq.

2) Improving Quality of Life
    Obama failed to make any serious efforts to curtail domestic terrorism in the United States, allowing suspected terrorists to operate freely. His anti-business bias, exemplified by the Affordable Care Act, or "Obamacare," stifled free enterprise and held back a true recovery from recession for the entire length of the Obama administration, until the results of the 2016 presidential and congressional elections were announced and it became apparent that the pro-business (and pro-employee) philosophy of the new Trump Administration would be in place soon.

3) Meeting Crises
    Several terrorist attacks on American facilities abroad left the United States government with only unanswered questions. Despite federal government expenditures in the trillions of dollars via various "stimulus" programs, the United States economy remained flat throughout the Obama presidency.

4) Overcoming Opposition
    Obama easily overcame opposition within the Democratic Party by appointing Hillary Clinton to be his Secretary of State and political heir-apparent. Republicans nominated soft, left-leaning candidates to oppose Obama in the 2008 and 2012 presidential elections; these candidates failed to earn the support of the more conservative members of the Republican Party, allowing Obama to coast to easy victories.

Obama's rating:

CATEGORY	VALUE	RATING
1) Making America Great	10	10%
2) Improving Quality of Life	8	20%
3) Meeting Crises	10	30%
4) Overcoming Opposition	8	40%

Total rating: 8.8

CHAPTER 11 – THE BAD PRESIDENTS

A very few presidents have had such a negative effect on the welfare of the country that they can be called "bad." The worst, of course, are James Buchanan and Franklin Pierce, whose actions led directly to the Civil War. Every poll of mainstream historians or other experts lists these two near or at the bottom in presidential rankings.

42) Lyndon Johnson, Democrat
Lyndon Johnson was a typical southern politician, although he had stronger ties to the New Deal of Franklin Roosevelt than most southerners. He became the Senate majority leader in the 1950s, but was still considered a southern Democrat. He came to the conclusion at that time that the increased wealth of the average American was turning the "mainstream" against the Democratic Party and more toward the Republicans, and felt that to maintain their dominant position in American politics the Democrats had to find new voters, lots of them. He seized upon the largely unenfranchised black population of the country as an excellent source of new Democrat voters, and began to court them. After becoming president in 1963 with the assassination of John F. Kennedy, Johnson began a massive program of enhanced welfare benefits, targeting African Americans as the primary beneficiaries. This, combined with the increased cost of the massive build-up of the Viet Nam War after the Tonkin Gulf Resolution, required large tax increases while still increasing the federal deficit. These actions, combined with the anti-Goldwater rhetoric of Johnson's 1964 presidential

campaign, were the beginning of the increased ideological split between the two major political parties in the United States.

Regarding the qualities by which the presidents are evaluated, Lyndon Johnson fares as follows:

1) Making America Great

   Lyndon Johnson used the alleged attack by North Vietnamese torpedo boats against United States Navy destroyers in the Gulf of Tonkin to push for expanded American involvement in Viet Nam, resulting eventually in the deaths of more than 50,000 American soldiers without a victory in sight, while the prestige and respect for the United States plummeted around the world. Johnson was accused of imperialism when he sent United States troops into the Dominican Republic to put down a revolt against their government.

2) Improving Quality of Life

   Lyndon Johnson's promises to black people, dubbed the "War on Poverty" were slow to be fulfilled, resulting in massive race riots and the destruction of large portions of several major, and smaller, cities around the United States. Federal troops had to be sent in to Detroit in 1967 to restore order. In 1968, Johnson had to call out federal troops to Washington, D.C., to put down race riots. Eventually Johnson got Congress to vote for federal aid to education and for medical care for senior citizens. The Department of Housing and Urban Development and the Department of Transportation were created during Johnson's presidency.

3) Meeting Crises

   Protests against Lyndon Johnson's Viet Nam policy grew, combined with race riots, forcing him to call out federal troops to put down riots in Washington, D.C.

4) Overcoming Opposition

   Lyndon Johnson was unable to overcome increasing opposition to his policies, especially his handling of the Viet Nam war, and he eventually had to decline nomination as the Democratic Party candidate for president in 1968.

Lyndon Johnson's rating:

CATEGORY	VALUE	RATING
1) Making America Great	10	20%
2) Improving Quality of Life	8	30%
3) Meeting Crises	10	10%
4) Overcoming Opposition	8	30%

Total rating: 7.8

43) Andrew Jackson, Democrat

Andrew Jackson was the last Revolutionary War veteran to achieve the Presidency, and the only president to have been a prisoner-of-war. Jackson, true to his Scotch-Irish heritage, was highly opinionated, quick to take offense, and very prejudiced. He was no friend to either the native Indians or to blacks, slave or free, as his actions and policies showed. He was very strongly patriotic, having "won" the War of 1812 almost singlehandedly by the Battle of New Orleans, although that battle was irrelevant, having actually been fought after the war was officially over and a peace treaty had been signed. Jackson took the side of Union as opposed to State's Rights in the Nullification Crisis of 1832, while correctly foretelling that the state's rights issue would rise again on the slavery question.

Regarding the qualities by which the presidents are evaluated, Jackson fares as follows:

1) Making America Great

   Andrew Jackson appointed his henchman, Roger B. Taney, as Chief Justice of the Supreme Court after Taney successfully transferred federal funds to Jackson's "pet" banks. Taney pushed the Dred Scott Decision through the Court, declaring that negroes had no political rights anywhere in the United States, whether they were slave or free. This unleashed a political firestorm across the country. It was the opening step to Civil War.

2) Improving Quality of Life

   Jackson decided to put the Bank of the United States out of business, as a means of ruining his political enemy, Nicholas Biddle. The Bank of the United States was the only financial institution providing stability to the currency system in the United States. When Jackson issued his Specie Circular, requiring only gold to be used in payments to the United States Treasury, the economy took a downturn. Without the financial stability provided by the Bank of the United States, a severe depression soon came, although it did not make its heaviest mark until the following Van Buren Administration. Jackson was an energetic supporter of westward expansion at the expense of the natives. He failed to honor Indian treaties, even those he negotiated.

3) Meeting Crises

   In the case of Cherokee Nation vs. Georgia Jackson refused to enforce a decision by John Marshall's Supreme Court stating that the Indians were "domestic dependent nations" and had a right to their property until they voluntarily ceded it. Jackson reportedly said "John Marshall has made his decision, now let him enforce it." The decision was never enforced and the Cherokees were eventually forced to leave their land. During the Nullification crisis, Jackson bullied the leader of the nullification party, John C. Calhoun, into backing down. While this was a positive result, Jackson was, in fact, a personal enemy of Calhoun's and welcomed the opportunity to humiliate him. Considering Jackson's career, he may not have been a true opponent of nullification to the extent the incident with Calhoun suggests. At the risk of war, Jackson pressured France to make payments for damages done to American shipping during the Napoleonic wars, resolving the issue and resulting in resumption of good relations with France. Jackson recognized Texas independence on his last day in office, leaving to his successors the resolution of the issue of annexation of Texas.

4) Overcoming Opposition

   Jackson had many powerful enemies and single-handedly caused the Whig Party to be created more as an anti-Jackson party than for any other political purpose (the Whigs originated in England as the party opposing the power of the king, and favoring Parliament). The Whigs tended to be primarily a party of the financially and socially elite, while Jackson's followers coalesced into what they began to call the Democratic Party, representing, in Jackson's words regarding the bank war, "…the humble members of society, the farmers, mechanics, and laborers…" Jackson was victorious for a time, but his hand-picked successor went down to crashing defeat in his bid for reelection after the results of Jackson's policies became apparent.

Jackson's rating:

CATEGORY	VALUE	RATING
1) Making America Great	10	30%
2) Improving Quality of Life	8	15%
3) Meeting Crises	10	20%
4) Overcoming Opposition	8	10%

Total rating: 7.0

44) James Buchanan, Democrat

James Buchanan was a career Pennsylvania politician, but he was also instrumental in early railroad development in the United States, having been a promoter and builder of the Harrisburg, Portsmouth, Mount Joy, and Lancaster Railroad in the 1830s, a line that eventually formed a key part of the Pennsylvania Railroad system. Buchanan was a highly experienced politician having served at different levels in the executive and legislative branches of government for many years; he was 65 years old when sworn in as president.

James Buchanan is generally recognized as one of the worst of the United States presidents, due to his desperate efforts to satisfy the demands of the slave states prior to the Civil War. The only justification for his actions is that he was attempting to prevent secession. The fact remains that his activities, and the activities of some of his subordinates, can be technically characterized as treason.

Regarding the qualities by which the presidents are evaluated, Buchanan fares as follows:

1) Making America Great

Buchanan tried and failed to purchase Alaska from Russia and Cuba from Spain. Further lowering American prestige internationally, he enthusiastically welcomed Chief Justice Taney's Dred Scott Decision, fomenting monumental outrage throughout the North and encouraging the slavocracy in the South.

2) Improving Quality of Life

Buchanan attempted to force admission of Kansas as a slave state to minimize the majority held in the Senate by the free states since the admission of California in 1850, followed by Minnesota and Oregon, all free states, so that the Senate consisted of 36 members from free states and 30 from slave states by 1860, with other potential free states and no potential slave states in the wings. His efforts failed but resulted in "Bloody Kansas."

3) Meeting Crises

Buchanan disclaimed responsibility for secession, but actually, through his Secretary of War, aided the South in weaponizing for rebellion. It is believed by some that this action made Buchanan liable for impeachment on the grounds of treason. He claimed a lack of authority to resist the secession of southern states but readily sent federal troops to put down the anti-U.S. rebellion among the Mormons in Utah Territory.

4) Overcoming Opposition

Buchanan waived the possibility of running for a second term shortly after his election, resulting in immediate lame-duck status, with the leadership of the Democratic Party falling to Stephen A. Douglas of Illinois. Buchanan's departure from the presidency ended his participation in politics, as he spent most of the remainder of his life defending himself from accusations of assisting the South and helping to start the Civil War.

Buchanan's rating:

CATEGORY	VALUE	RATING
1) Making America Great	10	25%
2) Improving Quality of Life	8	5%
3) Meeting Crises	10	20%
4) Overcoming Opposition	8	20%

Total rating: 6.5

45) Franklin Pierce, Democrat

Franklin Pierce, although a New England Yankee (from New Hampshire), was pro-south and pro-slavery. His main goal as president, in keeping with Democratic Party policy, was to keep the South happy and particularly to even out representation in the Senate so that at least half its members would be from slave states and no more than half from free states. Pierce attempted to buy Mexico and Cuba to form more slave states, while rejecting the annexation of Hawaii as it would have been likely to become a free state. His signature on the Kansas-Nebraska Act guaranteed the coming of the Civil War as it was totally unacceptable to the Northern population, and considered a necessity by the South. On the positive side, Pierce was in the White House when a trade treaty with Japan was negotiated, and he promoted the Atlantic cable and land grants for railroads.

Franklin Pierce is generally recognized as one of the worst of the United States presidents. Pierce was perfectly willing to allow the entire United States to become slave territory in order to satisfy the demands of southern slaveholders. His complete lack of concern for the welfare of the slave population, and for the future of the unskilled and semiskilled portion of the free population of the country in a slavery-dominated society, justifies labeling him as the worst of United States presidents.

Regarding the qualities by which the presidents are evaluated, Pierce fares as follows:

1) Making America Great

As president, Pierce strongly supported the Compromise of 1850, a blatantly pro-slavery measure that included the Fugitive Slave Act that severely restricted the rights of African Americans.

2) Improving Quality of Life
    Pierce signed the Kansas-Nebraska Act, nullifying the Missouri Com-
    promise and opening the entire western territories to slavery. This ig-
    nited a firestorm of opposition in the North that led directly to the
    secession of several slave states and to the Civil War, in which more
    than half a million Americans died.

3) Meeting Crises
    In order to cool the increasing furor of the slave states over Northern
    opposition, Pierce attempted to buy Cuba from Spain, to prevent the
    freeing of its slaves and thereby avert a slave rebellion in the United
    States, as well as to form another slave state. He also refused admis-
    sion to Hawaii, which would have been a free state. His Cuba efforts
    failed.

4) Overcoming Opposition
    Pierce, in spite of wanting to continue in office, was rejected as the
    Democrat candidate for the 1856 presidential election due to oppo-
    sition from northern Democrats. In spite of having some support as
    the Democrat candidate for President in 1860, Pierce chose to retire
    from electoral politics.

Pierce's rating:

CATEGORY	VALUE	RATING
1) Making America Great	10	20%
2) Improving Quality of Life	8	10%
3) Meeting Crises	10	10%
4) Overcoming Opposition	8	15%

Total rating: 5.0

There are, as indicated above and further detailed in Chapter 14, many factors
that enter into the evaluation of a president of the United States, whether for
ranking purposes or simple assessment of a presidency. One factor that can be
determined for each president, independent of his cohorts, is presidential

strength. Some presidents thrive on adversity, others meet a challenge with the effort required to overcome it. Other presidents may fail to overcome barriers or may lead the country in a direction that was unwisely chosen. Other presidents may use their overwhelming popularity to justify actions that, perhaps in retrospect, were unwise. Still other presidents, due to being very unpopular, had difficulty in achieving worthy goals, or may in fact have failed at them.

The following table lists the presidents in 1) chronological order, 2) with their Real Ranking (highest to lowest), and 3) in decreasing order of strength (strongest to weakest), with party affiliation:

PRESIDENT CHRONOLOGICALLY		PRESIDENT REAL RANKING	PRESIDENTIAL STRENGTH	PARTY
1	WASHINGTON	1 WASHINGTON	1 JACKSON	DEM
2	J. ADAMS	2 LINCOLN	2 WILSON	DEM
3	JEFFERSON	3 REAGAN	3 REAGAN	REP
4	MADISON	4 JEFFERSON	4 T. ROOSEVELT	REP
5	MONROE	5 J. ADAMS	5 JEFFERSON	DEM*
6	J. Q. ADAMS	6 POLK	6 F. D. ROOSEVELT	DEM
7	JACKSON	7 T. ROOSEVELT	7 TRUMAN	DEM
8	VAN BUREN	8 EISENHOWER	8 EISENHOWER	REP
9	W. H. HARRISON	9 NIXON	9 LINCOLN	REP
10	TYLER	10 G. H. W. BUSH	10 POLK	DEM
11	POLK	11 ARTHUR	11 WASHINGTON	REP*
12	TAYLOR	12 MCKINLEY	12 NIXON	REP
13	FILLMORE	13 TAFT	13 L. JOHNSON	DEM
14	PIERCE	14 HOOVER	14 J. ADAMS	REP*
15	BUCHANAN	15 COOLIDGE	15 TRUMP	REP
16	LINCOLN	16 FORD	16 MONROE	DEM*
17	A. JOHNSON	17 MONROE	17 OBAMA	DEM
18	GRANT	18 J. Q. ADAMS	18 HAYES	REP
19	HAYES	19 TAYLOR	19 TAYLOR	REP*
20	GARFIELD	20 HAYES	20 TYLER	DEM
21	ARTHUR	21 B. HARRISON	21 CLEVELAND (1)	DEM
22	CLEVELAND (1)	22 GARFIELD	22 PIERCE	DEM
23	B. HARRISON	23 TRUMP	23 ARTHUR	REP
24	CLEVELAND (2)	24 W. H. HARRISON	24 CLEVELAND (2)	DEM
25	MCKINLEY	25 CLEVELAND (1)	25 G. W. BUSH	REP
26	T. ROOSEVELT	26 CLEVELAND (2)	26 TAFT	REP
27	TAFT	27 G. W. BUSH	27 COOLIDGE	REP
28	WILSON	28 GRANT	28 HOOVER	REP
29	HARDING	29 HARDING	29 J. Q. ADAMS	REP*
30	COOLIDGE	30 FILLMORE	30 A. JOHNSON	DEM
31	HOOVER	31 A. JOHNSON	31 MCKINLEY	REP
32	F. D. ROOSEVELT	32 TYLER	32 GRANT	REP
33	TRUMAN	33 VAN BUREN	33 KENNEDY	DEM
34	EISENHOWER	34 CARTER	34 CLINTON	DEM
35	KENNEDY	35 F. D. ROOSEVELT	35 FILLMORE	REP*
36	L. JOHNSON	36 TRUMAN	36 HARDING	REP
37	NIXON	37 CLINTON	37 G. H. W. BUSH	REP
38	FORD	38 KENNEDY	38 BUCHANAN	DEM
39	CARTER	39 MADISON	39 B. HARRISON	REP
40	REAGAN	40 WILSON	40 VAN BUREN	DEM
41	G. H. W. BUSH	41 OBAMA	41 GARFIELD	REP
42	CLINTON	42 L. JOHNSON	42 FORD	REP
43	G. W. BUSH	43 JACKSON	43 CARTER	DEM
44	OBAMA	44 BUCHANAN	44 MADISON	DEM*
45	TRUMP	45 PIERCE	45 W. H. HARRISON	REP*

* Party indicated is modern equivalent of party affiliation at the time of presidency, overt or implied

TABLE 11-1 PRESIDENTS, RANKING, STRENGTH

While there is considerable material available in this volume to justify the Real Rankings in the above table, the strength ranking of the presidents is admittedly much more subjective. Presidential strength can change within a presidential term, as popularity or other factors can change radically. While a general grouping of strong, weak and moderate presidents can be fairly easily obtained, ranking all 45 presidents (counting Cleveland twice) can be difficult. The difference in ranking of the presidents by multiple evaluators under this criterion would possibly show even more variation than the differences in ranking seen in the 19 different presidential rankings illustrated in Wikipedia (see Chapter 14), but "strong" vs "weak" transcends party affiliation, at least to some extent, so political bias would be a lesser factor in a strength ranking.

CHAPTER 12 — THE POPULARITY CONTEST I

Some good presidents were also popular, but dying in office generally does more for a president's popularity than good performance. Popular vote is also not a good leading indicator for either popularity or good performance. Some of the presidents with the highest percentage of the popular vote ended up least popular, and some performed poorly. In general, presidents perform better in popularity than Congress or the Press, but there have been exceptions. Regardless of who or what is responsible for good times or bad, the president usually gets the credit or the blame. People generally remember the good times and forget the bad times, so many presidents have a higher degree of popularity than they perhaps should hold.

Some of the presidents most popular throughout their terms were Democrats: John Kennedy, Franklin Delano Roosevelt, Bill Clinton, and Barrack Obama possibly all could have been elected for life; Kennedy and FDR were. In all these cases, their key virtue was expressed sympathy for the plight of the common man or the poor, regardless of whether they accomplished anything material to improve the lives of such persons. Such a persona is truly a valuable asset for a politician running for office in a democracy. The "I feel your pain" mantra of Bill Clinton assured him eternal high popularity numbers in spite of his lackluster, even scandalous, presidency. In fact, all of the most popular presidents representing the Democratic Party after 1900 were progressives, whose main vote-getting mechanism was the promise of redistribution of wealth, as opposed to increasing prosperity for all.

The popular vote is not necessarily a reflection on the popularity of a president, as the popular vote can be, and often is, a vote against someone or something. Warren Harding's high popular vote total in 1920 was more a vote against Woodrow Wilson, or Woodrow Wilson's policies, and a statement of dissatisfaction with the aftermath of World War I, than a positive statement about Warren Harding. Richard Nixon's popular vote in 1972 was as much or more against George McGovern and his expressed liberal political philosophy than a positive endorsement of Richard Nixon.

The most unpopular presidents were John Quincy Adams, Andrew Johnson, and Herbert Hoover. Their unpopularity was mostly due to political opposition that was assisted by a hostile Press. Hoover became what could be called the mirror image of William Clinton, being perceived as completely unsympathetic to the plight of the poor in spite of his initiation of many assistance programs at the start of the Great Depression of the 1930s.

Several presidents started out with high popularity but lost it by the time their terms were over. These include Warren Harding, Richard Nixon, and Jimmy Carter.

Some of the most unpopular presidents were those who were elected president without gaining a majority or even a plurality of the popular vote. Two early presidents were elected without obtaining a majority of the electoral vote; they were chosen by the House of Representatives. Thomas Jefferson, in 1800, tied with Aaron Burr in the Electoral College. As Jefferson was the intended president and Burr was the intended vice president, there was little opposition to Jefferson's selection as president by the House. It was recognized almost immediately that Burr's numerical electoral tie with Jefferson was due to a constitutional flaw; this was soon remedied by the 12th Amendment. Burr's failure to willingly cede the presidency to Jefferson caused him severe public censure, and Burr eventually became a renegade. On the other hand, in 1824, when Andrew Jackson, John Quincy Adams, Henry Clay, and William Crawford split the electoral vote, and the president was chosen by the House of Representatives from the three candidates with the highest vote totals, Jackson, Adams, and Clay, the Jackson people complained long and bitterly when the House chose Adams over Jackson in spite of Jackson having a plurality of the electoral vote. Adams was hounded throughout his presidency and received no cooperation from Congress for his proposals, and received a crushing defeat at the hands of Jackson in the ensuing presidential election of 1828.

A few other presidents were elected with a majority of the electoral vote while not receiving a majority of the popular vote. Three of these presidents, Benjamin Harrison, George W. Bush, and Donald Trump, were clearly the winners based on the rules set out in the Constitution, but the supporters of the losing candidates (Democrats in every case), who received more popular votes than the winners, never ceased complaining. Proposals have been made to change the method of electing the president to more closely follow the popular vote, but the extra two electoral votes for each state, which were insisted upon by the smaller states at the time of adoption of the Constitution, remain and are likely to continue, in spite of the United States today being more of a nation than the confederacy it was when the Constitution was adopted. The smaller states were, as a rule, quick to ratify the Constitution, Delaware, New Jersey, and Georgia ratifying unanimously at their conventions, while two of the largest states at the time, Virginia and New York, hesitated until the ninth ratification (by New Hampshire) put it into effect, and then joined the new Union. The smaller states in 1787-88, except for cantankerous Rhode Island, were happy to join the Union, primarily because of the equal representation in the Senate and corresponding extra weight in selection of the president, and the same would undoubtedly hold true today if an attempt were made to eliminate this feature of the Constitution.

Looking at all the elections in which the winner did not receive a majority of the popular vote, the number of changes in the person of the elected President that would have occurred if the popular vote were decisive might not favor one party:

Election Year	Winner	Percent of Popular Vote (excluding vote for minor candidates)
1824	John Quincy Adams	31.8%
1848	Zachary Taylor	47.3%
1856	James Buchanan	45.3%
1860	Abraham Lincoln	45.0%
1876	Rutherford B. Hayes	48.5%
1888	Benjamin Harrison	49.6%
1892	Grover Cleveland	47.2%
1912	Woodrow Wilson	45.3%
1948	Harry Truman	49.9%
1968	Richard Nixon	43.6%
1992	William Clinton	43.3%
2000	George W. Bush	48.4%
2016	Donald Trump	46.8%

See pages 138-141 for more detail on these elections. Five Democrats and seven Republicans were minority-popular-vote winners, and the thirteenth, John Quincy Adams, ran under the same party banner, "Republican"*, as all the other major candidates in that election. In some cases, as with Taylor, Cleveland, Truman, Nixon, and Trump, a third candidate's votes probably would have gone to the winner if the third-party candidate (See Appendix B) had not run, giving the winner a majority of the popular vote. On the other hand, John Quincy Adams, James Buchanan, Abraham Lincoln, Rutherford B. Hayes, Benjamin Harrison, Woodrow Wilson, William Clinton, and George W. Bush were clearly not the choice of the majority of voters. Therefore three Democrats and four Republicans, and one pre-1856 "Republican"*, were chosen by a minority of the voters. Two, Hayes and Benjamin Harrison, defeated a candidate who received a majority of the popular vote.

There has frequently been agitation for term limits for elected politicians, and after Franklin Delano Roosevelt's presidency a Constitutional Amendment, the twenty-second, to limit presidents to no more than two full terms, plus two years of a preceding president's term, was adopted. There is still heard occasionally a call for a single presidential term of six years. If this were in effect, it would not change the length of the average president's term much, as it is, as of 2020, a little over five years. Unfortunately, it would deprive the country of the full services of that rare president who could fill a much longer term to the satisfaction of an overwhelming majority of the people. It also would produce instant lame-duck status, reducing the President's stature in the governmental triumvirate. If there was no limitation on presidential terms, a few presidents could have been reelected for life, or until they decided to retire for medical or other physical reasons; some perhaps should have been.

Several presidents were elected for life, albeit inadvertently: William Henry Harrison, Zachary Taylor, Abraham Lincoln, James A. Garfield, William McKinley, Warren G. Harding, Franklin Delano Roosevelt, and John Fitzgerald Kennedy all died in office. Lincoln, Garfield, McKinley, and Kennedy were assassinated, the others, Harrison, Taylor (presumably), Harding (presumably), and Roosevelt died of natural causes. Several other presidents died shortly after leaving office, so that if they were reelected they would not

---

*The party of Thomas Jefferson, not the party of Abraham Lincoln.

have lasted long. There are a few presidents who most likely could have been reelected as long as they wanted to serve, or until they died in office: George Washington, Andrew Jackson, Abraham Lincoln, U.S. Grant, William McKinley, Franklin Delano Roosevelt, Dwight Eisenhower, John F. Kennedy, and Ronald Reagan. Republicans Eisenhower, McKinley, Grant, Lincoln, and Reagan all increased their popular vote on reelection over their initial winning vote. Democrat Andrew Jackson had lower popular vote totals for reelection than for his initial election; Franklin Delano Roosevelt increased his popular vote percentage for his first reelection, in 1936, but his vote percentage dwindled thereafter.

Vote-getting power is not a sure means of determining the best president according to experts' standards. Some of the presidents with the highest winning percentage of the popular vote left office in disgrace, such as Warren Harding, Lyndon Johnson, and Richard Nixon; or lost their reelection bid: Martin Van Buren.

Of the 45 presidents to date, counting Cleveland twice, only twenty have been elected as sitting presidents: Washington, Jefferson, Madison, Monroe, Jackson, Lincoln, Grant, McKinley, Theodore Roosevelt (only elected once), Wilson, Coolidge (only elected once), Franklin Roosevelt (reelected three times), Truman (only elected once), Eisenhower, Lyndon Johnson (only elected once), Nixon, Reagan, Clinton, George W. Bush, and Obama. Ten Republicans and ten Democrats, an even split. Only twelve served a full two terms (or more, in the case of FDR), and one of these, Wilson, was an at least partly incapacitated invalid for the last year and a half of his presidency. Of the nine perpetually popular presidents listed above, five are listed in the top third in the Real Ranking, one in the middle third, and three are in the bottom third. In a comparison of the four ranking systems cited in Chapter 14, six are placed in the top third, and three are placed in the middle third, except seven are in the top third, one in the middle third and one in the bottom third in one poll.

CHAPTER 13 – THE POPULARITY CONTEST II

The popular vote in a Presidential election in the United States is largely a popularity contest. The person with the best publicity and the most charming persona almost always wins. Anyone who has been championing an unpopular program, such as raising taxes, or is blamed for a disaster of some sort, usually loses.

The winners of the popular vote, their percentages, and their denouement, are as follows, in decreasing order, winners prior to 1824, when the popular vote was not tabulated, are not included even though the results of those elections were in some cases remarkable: 100% of the electoral vote twice, for George Washington, who faced no opposition in either election; 99.6% once, for James Monroe (no opposition, he would have received 100% but one elector voted against his state's vote), 92% once, for Jefferson.

Warren G Harding (R), 1920, 63.8%
Harding died in office, possibly of food poisoning, perhaps a heart attack and pneumonia; some say suicide, some suggested murder, after the malfeasance of some of his cabinet members was beginning to become known, at least to him. The 1920 presidential vote may have been a protest against the Wilson Administration.

Franklin Delano Roosevelt (D), 1936, 62.5%
FDR had convinced people, during his first term, that he had their best interests at heart in fighting the Great Depression of the 1930s. The worst of the Depression was, in fact, over by the election of 1936. Roosevelt went on to win a third and a fourth term, although with lesser percentages of the popular vote.

Richard Nixon (R), 1972, 61.8%

This was largely a protest against the perceived socialist policies of Nixon's opponent, George McGovern. Not unlike the 1964 election (see below) the public's perception of the losing candidate was largely the result of the negative campaign tactics of the winner. Nixon may have also benefitted by the "dirty tricks" of the Committee to Reelect the President, including the notorious Watergate break-in, which eventually did him in.

Lyndon Johnson (D), 1964, 61.3%

Johnson had an opponent in 1964, Barry Goldwater, who seemed by many to be promising a nuclear holocaust if elected. The Johnson campaign seized on this, portraying Goldwater as a warmonger, with a lurid advertising campaign, and won the election handily. Johnson went on to massively escalate the Viet Nam war, resulting in tens of thousands of deaths of American soldiers, but with no clear sign of victory, and declined to run for an additional term, as his popularity declined to near zero in 1968.

Theodore Roosevelt (R), 1904, 60.6%

After succeeding the assassinated William McKinley in 1901, Teddy Roosevelt achieved tremendous popularity as a "trust buster" and as the very popular jingoistic builder of the Panama Canal. He declined to run again in 1908, stating that he had already served the traditional maximum 2 terms (including almost all of McKinley's second term). He changed his mind in 1912 but could not get the Republican nomination due to his reputation as a more than moderate progressive. He ran in 1912 as a third-party progressive "Bull Moose" candidate, throwing the election to the Democrat, Woodrow Wilson. Roosevelt reversed himself on progressivism before he died in 1919.

Ronald Reagan (R), 1984, 59.2%

After being ridiculed as an actor-politician in his first term, Reagan showed himself a strong president with lots of ideas on how to improve the lot of the America people, cruising to an easy victory in 1984 with 97.6% of the electoral vote. His popularity continued in spite of some scandals in his second term, and he probably could have been elected for life.

Franklin Delano Roosevelt (D), 1932, 59.1%

Herbert Hoover was widely blamed for 1) not avoiding the Great Depression, which began in Hoover's first year in office, and 2) for not doing enough to combat the Great Depression after its effects were felt. An easy victory in 1932 took little effort on Roosevelt's part, and he was easily reelected three times.

Herbert Hoover (R), 1928, 58.8%

The nation was prosperous, World War I was largely forgotten, people felt the best way to keep things as they were was to vote for Herbert Hoover in 1928, the candidate of the party that had been in control of the government for the last seven+ years. The 1929 stock market crash quickly ended his popularity.

Martin Van Buren (D), 1836, 58.2%

Van Buren was the anointed successor to the people's hero, Andrew Jackson. It was fairly well known that Van Buren was the "brains" behind the Jackson presidency. His main competitor in 1836 was William Henry Harrison. If the vote of minor candidates, when Van Buren's opponents, the Whigs, strategized that different Whig candidates should run in different parts of the country where they were most popular, are included, Van Buren's percentage of the vote is only 50.9%. He later lost reelection handily.

Dwight Eisenhower (R), 1956, 56.0%

Eisenhower was an extremely popular president. His experience as Commander of Allied Forces in Europe, and as head of NATO, the North Atlantic Treaty Organization, gave people confidence in his abilities; his performance in his first term gave little reason to doubt those abilities and he was easily reelected.

Andrew Jackson (D), 1828, 56.0%

Jackson had been campaigning hard for four years, since his loss to John Quincy Adams in the House of Representatives in 1824-5. His consistent, constant, complaint that he was the choice of the people, by virtue of his plurality of the 1824 popular vote, paid off.

Andrew Jackson (D), 1832, 55.0%

Jackson's vote percentage dropped slightly from 1828. His vote total increased slightly, by about 6 percent, while the country's population increased about 13 percent.

Dwight Eisenhower (R), 1952, 55.4%

Eisenhower was a popular war hero and career military man with a very clean record; the previous administration had been tainted with scandal, and there was public unrest arising from a variety of sources. Eisenhower was perceived to be a statesman unsullied by political dealings.

Abraham Lincoln (R), 1864, 55.1%

After a shaky first three years, Lincoln's presidency was doing well and it was clear that the Union armies were on the way to victory.

On the other end of the scale, several presidents won the Electoral College while obtaining less than 50% of the popular vote. Some of these elections had three or more major candidates, so that the winner may have had a plurality of the popular vote.

John Quincy Adams (NR), 1824, 31.8%

This was a four-man race, with Andrew Jackson, Henry Clay, and William Crawford also participating. All were prominent public figures. The three highest electoral vote getters went on to a race, per the Constitution, in the House of Representatives, where the vote was by state. In what was called a "corrupt bargain" by the supporters of Andrew Jackson, Henry Clay threw his support to Adams, who then won the vote in the House, and subsequently appointed Henry Clay as Secretary of State. There was nothing illegal or immoral about this, but Adams was hounded by Jackson supporters throughout his presidency and was not able to get any of his programs through Congress.

William Clinton (D), 1992, 43.3%

This was a three-man race, with Clinton obtaining a plurality of the popular vote and a clear majority of the electoral vote.

Richard Nixon 1968 (R), 43.6

This was a three-man race, with Nixon obtaining a plurality of the popular vote and a clear majority of the electoral vote. The third party candidate (George Wallace)'s vote probably would have largely gone to Nixon if it was only a two-man race, or those voters would have stayed home, so Nixon would have had a majority of the popular vote as well as the electoral vote.

Abraham Lincoln (R), 1860, 45.0%

This was a four-man race, with Lincoln obtaining a plurality of the popular vote and a clear majority of the electoral vote. It is quite possible that, if the southern Democrat candidate had stayed out of the election, the northern Democrat, Stephen A. Douglas, would have won most of his votes, but Lincoln still would have won the electoral vote.

Woodrow Wilson (D), 1912, 45.3%

This was a three-man race, with Wilson obtaining a plurality of the popular vote and a clear majority of the electoral vote. The Republican candidate, William Howard Taft, and the Bull Moose (Progressive) Party candidate, Theodore Roosevelt, split the conservative vote so that if only one of them was running he most likely would have won the election and Wilson would have been defeated.

James Buchanan (D), 1856, 45.3%

This was a three-man race, with Buchanan obtaining a plurality of the popular vote and a clear majority of the electoral vote. Together, John C. Fremont of the new Republican Party and Millard Fillmore, a former Whig running under the American Party banner, garnered a large majority of the popular vote. It is probable that, if Fillmore had not run, Fremont would have taken most of his vote and won the election easily.

Grover Cleveland (D), 1892, 47.2%

This was a three-man race, with Cleveland obtaining a plurality of the popular vote and a clear majority of the electoral vote. The votes of the third party's candidate, James Weaver of the populist or people's party, would likely have gone to Cleveland or those voters would have stayed home, so

Cleveland's percentage of the popular vote would have been higher if it was a two-man race.

Zachary Taylor (W), 1848, 47.3%

This was a three-man race, with Taylor obtaining a plurality of the popular vote and a clear majority of the electoral vote. The third-party candidate, Martin Van Buren, was running under the Free-Soil Party banner. As Van Buren was a former Democrat, it is difficult to say whether he took votes away from Taylor or from Lewis Cass, the Democrat candidate. If all of Van Buren's votes went to Cass instead, which is unlikely, Cass would have had a clear majority of the popular vote and may have won the election.

George W. Bush (R), 2000, 48.4%

This was a very closely contested race, with Bush winning by a Supreme Court decision giving him the electoral votes of Florida in the infamous "chads" case.

Rutherford B. Hayes (R), 1876, 48.5%

This was a close election, with the electoral votes of two states in dispute. Hayes had to obtain all the disputed electoral votes to win, which he did. Most analysts conclude that Hayes' opponent was unfairly denied all or some of those electoral votes, so that Hayes should have lost the election.

Donald Trump (R), 2016, 46.8%

There were several candidates in this race who won substantial numbers of popular votes without winning any electoral votes. The plurality of popular votes was won by Hilary Clinton, the liberal or Democrat candidate, by about 65.9 million to 63 million, or 51.1 percent when counting only hers and Donald Trump's votes. A razor thin majority of the popular vote was won by conservative candidates over liberal candidates, approximately 67.6 million to 67.1 million, so that Clinton's share of the total presidential vote in 2016 was only 48.9 percent. Trump won 305 electoral votes, 56.7 percent, to 233 for Clinton.

Benjamin Harrison (R), 1888, 49.6%

Harrison, the Republican, defeated the Democrat candidate, the incumbent Grover Cleveland, in spite of losing the popular vote. Cleveland, the incumbent, was an unpopular conservative Democrat who opposed the free coinage of silver, a concept popular among many of the Democratic Party faithful, some of whom may have stayed away from the polls during the election of 1888.

Harry Truman (D), 1948, 49.9%

This was a four-man race, with Truman obtaining a plurality of the popular vote and a clear majority of the electoral vote. It was widely predicted that the unpopular incumbent, Truman, would lose the election, and many called the election for his Republican opponent, Thomas Dewey, before late returns gave the election to Truman.

Several presidents were elected with just over 50% of the popular vote, but less than 52-1/2%, so they could hardly be said to have a mandate. These include: U.S. Grant's 1st term, William McKinley's 1st term, Barrack Obama's 2nd term, Woodrow Wilson's 2nd term, Ronald Reagan's 1st term, George W. Bush's 2nd term, Jimmy Carter, Grover Cleveland's 1st and 2nd terms, John F. Kennedy, and James A. Garfield. Interestingly, however, Grant, McKinley, Reagan, and Bush, all Republicans, in their second election all improved their vote margins over their first election, while Obama and Cleveland, both Democrats, had a lower percentage of the popular vote in their second election as compared to their first.

The other side of the popularity coin is in the reelection contest. Sitting presidents usually have a tremendous advantage when they run for reelection, as they already have name recognition, and some sort of record to run on. Nevertheless, several sitting presidents have lost in their attempts at reelection. These include: John Adams, John Quincy Adams, Grover Cleveland, Benjamin Harrison, William Howard Taft, Herbert Hoover, Gerald Ford, Jimmy Carter, and George H.W. Bush, all but two of whom were Republicans. Gerald Ford was the only totally nonelected president, having replaced Spiro Agnew as vice president without facing an election after Agnew resigned, and then having been advanced from vice president when Richard M. Nixon resigned the presidency. Other vice presidents who attained the office of president upon the death of their predecessor, such as Chester Arthur, would have liked to run for president on their own but were denied the nomination by their party. A few ex-presidents, such as Millard Fillmore, who became president when Zachary Taylor died in office, and also Martin Van Buren and Theodore Roosevelt, ran, after their presidencies, as third party candidates but were defeated.

CHAPTER 14 – THE POPULARITY CONTEST III

The Typical Polls

Officially, Grover Cleveland is both the 22nd and 24th President. Most polls have combined his two terms to produce one ranking. Real Ranking has included Cleveland twice in its ranking, even though both ratings for Cleveland in Real Ranking are similar, so much so that Real Ranking places Grover Cleveland at #24 and #25 in the Presidential ranking, with ratings of 18.0 and 17.6, respectively.

There can be considered to be three schools of presidential rankings. The presidential ratings and resultant rankings detailed in this book can be considered to be from a conservative point of view. Most published rankings are more suited to a liberal philosophy of government, and value differently the properties and accomplishments of the presidents. Strict libertarians hold presidents to a much more rigid standard of constitutionality, and their presidential ratings bear little resemblance to the others. In chapters twelve-fourteen are discussed the liberal school, as shown in the mainstream rankings as illustrated in Wikipedia, *Historical rankings of the presidents of the United States*. Then there is the conservative school, as enumerated here in Real Rankings in chapters 5-11. And finally there is the libertarian school, as propounded by Ivan Eland and others. The following table compares mainstream rankings as displayed in Wikipedia, the Real Rankings, and a libertarian ranking as compiled by Ivan Eland.

President	Mainstream Ranking**	Real Ranking	Eland Ranking
Washington	3	1	7
Adams	15	5	22
Jefferson	5	4	26
Madison	14	39	28
Monroe	17	17	25
John Quincy Adams	21	18	12
Jackson	9	43	27
Van Buren	24	33	3
William Henry Harrison	38 (11 votes)	24	no ranking
Tyler	37	32	1
Polk	12	6	38
Taylor	35	19	13
Fillmore	39	30	14
Pierce	40	45	24
Buchanan	43	44	23
Lincoln	1	2	29
Andrew Johnson	41	31	17
Grant	36	28	19
Hayes	25	20	4
Garfield	29 (11 votes)	22	no ranking
Arthur	28	11	5
Cleveland	20	25	2
Benjamin Harrison	31	21	15
Cleveland	20	26	2
McKinley	19	12	39
Theodore Roosevelt	4	7	21
Taft	23	13	20
Wilson	7	40	41
Harding	42	29	6
Coolidge	30	15	10
Hoover	34	14	18
Franklin Roosevelt	2	35	31
Truman	6 (18 votes)	36	40
Eisenhower	8 (18 votes)	8	9
Kennedy	10 (17 votes)	38	36
Lyndon Johnson	13 (17 votes)	42	32
Nixon	33 (17 votes)	9	30
Ford	26 (17 votes)	16	16
Carter	27 (17 votes)	34	8
Reagan	16 (15 votes)	3	35
George H.W. Bush	22 (14 votes)	10	33
Clinton	18 (13 votes)	37	11
George W. Bush	32 (8 votes)	27	37
Obama	11 (4 votes)	41	34
Trump	44 (1 vote)	23	no ranking

** 19 entities provided ranking votes but not all evaluated all 45 presidents

Only two presidents were ranked similarly in all three systems: Washington at 3, 1, and 7, respectively, and Eisenhower at 8, 8, and 9, respectively. Four other presidents, Monroe, John Quincy Adams, Taft, and Ford had rankings ranges of ten or less. All these presidents had in common a public perception as disinterested public servants, or even as statesmen. Only two presidents, Washington and Eisenhower, were ranked in the top ten by all three. On the other end of the scale, Pierce, Buchanan, and George W. Bush were ranked twenty-third or worse by all three systems. A few presidents had uniformly mediocre rankings, such as Ford with 26, 16, and 16, respectively, Taft with 23, 13, and 20, respectively, John Quincy Adams at 21, 18, and 12, respectively, and Monroe, 17, 17, and 25, respectively. For comparison of all rankings of all presidents, corrections must be made for Cleveland, Trump, William Henry Harrison, and Garfield, but these do not make a big difference. The mainstream rankings are a composite of several separate rankings, and not all include the more recent presidents, making for a serious disturbance in comparison of the ranking numbers.

The 2017 rankings by C-SPAN's Historians Survey on Presidential Leadership - they have not, as of April 2020, included Donald Trump in their rankings:

C-SPAN   Real Ranking, adjusted

#1   Abraham Lincoln   2
#2   George Washington   1
#3   Franklin D. Roosevelt   33
#4   Theodore Roosevelt   7
#5   Dwight D. Eisenhower   8
#6   Harry Truman   34
#7   Thomas Jefferson   4
#8   John F. Kennedy   36
#9   Ronald Reagan   3
#10 Lyndon Johnson   40
#11 Woodrow Wilson   38
#12 Barrack Obama   39
#13 James Monroe   17
#14 James K. Polk   6
#15 Bill Clinton   35
#16 William McKinley   12
#17 James Madison   37
#18 Andrew Jackson   41
#19 John Adams   5
#20 George H. W. Bush   10
#21 John Quincy Adams   18
#22 Ulysses S. Grant   26
#23 Grover Cleveland   24
#24 William Howard Taft   13
#25 Gerald Ford   16
#26 Jimmy Carter   32
#27 Calvin Coolidge   15
#28 Richard Nixon   9
#29 James A. Garfield   22
#30 Benjamin Harrison   21
#31 Zachary Taylor   19
#32 Rutherford B. Hayes   20
#33 George W. Bush   25
#34 Martin Van Buren   31
#35 Chester A. Arthur   11
#36 Herbert Hoover   14
#37 Millard Fillmore   28
#38 William Henry Harrison   23
#39 John Tyler   30
#40 Warren G. Harding   27
#41 Franklin Pierce   43
#42 Andrew Johnson   29
#43 James Buchanan   42

C-SPAN ranked Cleveland only once, while Real Ranking included him once for each of his two non-consecutive terms. In adjusting this comparison, C-SPAN and the Real Ranking, using the same numerology, have identical rankings for no president. The Real Ranking and C-SPAN did come within 5 points of each other on the ratings of fourteen presidents, which is remarkable considering the apparent difference in criteria, as discussed below. C-SPAN and the Real Ranking differed by 20 points or more on only eleven presidents. Not surprisingly, nine of the eleven are Democrats, all rated much higher by C-SPAN. The greatest difference was with Franklin D. Roosevelt and Lyndon Johnson, both of whom had international diplomacy problems, Johnson in Viet Nam and Roosevelt in his inability to thwart Joseph Stalin's gain of hegemony in Eastern Europe, and domestically, with Roosevelt's failure to end the Great Depression and Johnson's disregard of the effect of his spending policies on the United States economy. Both of these presidents were aggressive advocates for the poor, at the expense of the middle class, and their Democratic Party remains in that position today.

Newsweek in February 2018 (see www.newsweek.com/donald-trump-george-washington-jfk-fdr-best-us-presidents-worst-us-presidents) ranked the United States presidents on a scale of zero to 100. The data is from the American Political Science Association's poll of current and recent members, rating each president on a scale of 0 to 100 for: great=100, average = 50, failure = zero. These rankings are included in the Wikipedia group (see below). From best to worst:

NEWSWEEK (APSA)		APSA RATING	REAL RANKING (modified to match Newsweek's numerology)
#1	Abraham Lincoln	95.03	2
#2	George Washington	92.59	1
#3	Franklin D. Roosevelt	89.09	34
#4	Theodore Roosevelt	81.39	7
#5	Thomas Jefferson	79.54	4
#6	Harry Truman	75.15	35
#7	Dwight Eisenhower	74.03	8
#8	Barrack Obama	71.13	40
#9	Ronald Reagan	69.29	3
#10	Lyndon Johnson	69.06	41
#11	Woodrow Wilson	67.40	39
#12	James Madison	64.48	38
#13	Bill Clinton	64.25	36
#14	John Adams	63.24	5
#15	Andrew Jackson	62.16	42
#16	John Fitzgerald Kennedy	61.86	37
#17	George H. W. Bush	60.90	10
#18	James Monroe	60.74	17
#19	William McKinley	55.49	12
#20	James K. Polk	54.09	6
#21	Ulysses S. Grant	52.88	27
#22	William H. Taft	51.86	13
#23	John Quincy Adams	51.9	18
#24	Grover Cleveland	51.01	25
(Cleveland is rated once for both terms)			
#25	Gerald Ford	47.28	16
#26	Jimmy Carter	45.04	33
#27	Martin Van Buren	44.27	32
#28	Calvin Coolidge	42.23	15
#29	Rutherford B. Hayes	41.50	20
#30	George W. Bush	40.42	26
#31	Chester A. Arthur	39.9	11
#32	Benjamin Harrison	37.63	21
#33	Richard Nixon	37.18	9
#34	James A. Garfield	36.64	22
#35	Zachary Taylor	33.34	19
#36	Herbert Hoover	33.27	14
#37	John Tyler	31.46	31
#38	Millard Fillmore	27.71	29
#39	Warren G. Harding	25.26	28
#40	Andrew Johnson	24.91	30
#41	Franklin Pierce	23.25	44
#42	William Henry Harrison	19.02	24
#43	James Buchanan	15.09	43
#44	Donald Trump	12.0+	23

Only one president, James Buchanan, received the same ranking by *Newsweek*/APSA as by "Real Ranking". Like C-SPAN, APSA combined both of Cleveland's two non-consecutive terms to provide one ranking for him. For twelve presidents, the APSA ranking was within 5 marks of the Real Ranking. Thirteen presidents had APSA rankings that were twenty or more points away from the Real Ranking. Nine of these were Democrats, and four were Republicans. Like with C-SPAN, the major differences with rankings among the Democrats were with very popular presidents, and again, apparently, performance took a rear seat to public image or presentation in development of the ratings by APSA. APSA had a high rating for Barrack Obama, in spite of the lack of real accomplishments in his presidency. His rating by APSA, as with the ratings for Franklin Roosevelt and Lyndon Johnson, appear to owe more to his perceived efforts for poor people than what he accomplished, or failed to accomplish, for them or for the nation as a whole. In spite of their stated criteria, as elucidated on page 147, APSA seems to rank non-activist and unpopular presidents as failures, regardless of their acomplishments. Ignoring their last-place rating for Donald Trump, made only one year into his presidency, their worst rating was for James Buchanan, universally regarded as one of the worst presidents the United States ever had. Both Real Ranking and APSA put Buchanan second to last.

The C-SPAN 2017 survey of presidential historians determined their order to determine the rankings of the presidents. Donald Trump was not included in the survey as it was too early in his presidency to make meaningful evaluations. The advisors for C-SPAN rated each president (except Trump) on a scale of one to ten on ten different qualities of presidential leadership, with each quality given the same weight: Public Persuasion, Crisis Leadership, Economic Management, Moral Authority, International Relations, Administrative Skills, Relations with Congress, Vision/Setting an Agenda, Pursued Equal Justice for All, and Performance Within Context of Times (see www.c-span.org/presidentsurvey2017/). It is debatable whether each of these categories is equally important, but opinion would most likely be divided as to which categories are more important than others, so probably by consensus of the historians no differentiation was made. Pursued equal justice for all, Public persuasion, Moral authority, and Vision/Setting agenda could be factors at least partially confused with popularity.

As with APSA, Grover Cleveland received a combined rating by C-SPAN for his two non-consecutive terms as president. The C-SPAN Presidential Historians rankings, as shown on page 146, with points scored for each president:

#1	Abraham Lincoln	907
#2	George Washington	868
#3	Franklin D. Roosevelt	855
#4	Theodore Roosevelt	807
#5	Dwight D. Eisenhower	745
#6	Harry S. Truman	737
#7	Thomas Jefferson	727
#8	John F. Kennedy	722
#9	Ronald Reagan	691
#10	Lyndon B. Johnson	687
#11	Woodrow Wilson	683
#12	Barrack Obama	669
#13	James Monroe	646
#14	James K. Polk	637
#15	William J. Clinton	634
#16	William McKinley	627
#17	James Madison	610
#18	Andrew Jackson	609
#19	John Adams	604
#20	George H.W. Bush	596
#21	John Quincy Adams	590
#22	Ulysses S. Grant	557
#23	Grover Cleveland	640
#24	William Howard Taft	528
#25	Gerald R. Ford	509
#26	Jimmy Carter	506
#27	Calvin Coolidge	506
#28	Richard M. Nixon	486
#29	James A. Garfield	481
#30	Benjamin Harrison	462
#31	Zachary Taylor	458
#32	Rutherford B. Hayes	458
#33	George W. Bush	456
#34	Martin Van Buren	450
#35	Chester A. Arthur	446
#36	Herbert Hoover	416
#37	Millard Fillmore	394
#38	William Henry Harrison	383

#39	John Tyler	372
#40	Warren G. Harding	360
#41	Franklin Pierce	315
#42	Andrew Johnson	275
#43	James Buchanan	245

Only three of the APSA rankings vary by more than five places from the C-SPAN rankings: Polk (20th vs 14th, respectively), Van Buren (27th vs 34th, respectively), and Kennedy (16th vs 8th, respectively). James K. Polk and John F. Kennedy receive higher rankings from C-SPAN while Martin Van Buren receives a higher ranking from APSA. The C-SPAN ranking for Polk is closer to Real Ranking, the APSA rating for Kennedy is closer to Real Ranking, while the C-SPAN ranking for Van Buren is almost identical to Real Ranking (34 v. 33).

Of the ten C-SPAN criteria, two are not considered by Real Ranking: Administrative skills and performance with context of times. Economic management could be considered a part of Improving Quality of Life and International Relations is a part of Making America Great. Overcoming Opposition could consist of Public persuasion, Moral authority, Relations with Congress, and Vision/Setting Agenda. Just one evaluation category is rated by both C-SPAN and Real Ranking and can be directly compared: Crisis Leadership or Meeting Crises. The relative bias of these two systems of rating can be determined by comparing the value obtained in this category for each president by each system:

President (RR order)	C-SPAN Crisis Leadership	Real Ranking Meeting Crises	C-SPAN/Real Ranking Quotient
Washington	94.1	90	1.046
Lincoln	97.8	100	0.978
Reagan	74.1	80	0.926
Jefferson	72.4	60	1.207
J. Adams	62.8	70	0.897
Polk	73.8	70	1.054
T. Roosevelt	83.5	60	1.392
Eisenhower	82.3	60	1.372
Nixon	49.1	50	0.982
G. H. W. Bush	72.7	60	1.212
Arthur	42.8	50	0.856
McKinley	64.8	55	1.178
Taft	49.9	50	0.998
Hoover	29.7	75	0.396
Coolidge	46.8	50	0.936
Ford	53.6	55	0.975
Monroe	66.1	50	1.322
J. Q. Adams	54.1	40	1.353
Taylor	47.6	50	0.952
Hayes	45.7	50	0.914
B. Harrison	42.5	50	0.850
Garfield	44.1	50	0.882
(Trump)	NO RATING	50	NO COMPARISON
W. H. Harrison	32.7	50	0.654
Cleveland	54.7	60	0.912
(Cleveland)	REPEAT	60	0.912
G. W. Bush	52.3	40	1.308
Grant	58.7	40	1.468
Harding	32.1	20	1.605
Fillmore	42.4	45	0.942
A. Johnson	25.3	10	2.530
Tyler	40.1	40	1.003
Van Buren	41.1	40	1.028
Carter	40.0	35	1.143
F. D. Roosevelt	94.1	45	2.091
Truman	85.1	35	2.431
Clinton	61.5	25	2.460
Kennedy	79.4	10	7.940
Madison	60.4	10	6.040
Wilson	73.4	40	1.835
Obama	65.4	30	2.180
L. B. Johnson	59.7	10	5.970
Jackson	73.5	20	3.675
Buchanan	17.4	20	0.870
Pierce	26.9	10	2.690

A value of more than 1.000 in the Quotient column indicates that C-SPAN gave the particular president a higher score in crisis management than did Real Ranking. A value in the Quotient column of less than 1.000 indicates a Real Ranking score higher than that given by C-SPAN's historians. As can be readily seen, Real Ranking is more critical on crisis management, as, of the forty-four presidents compared, twenty-six presidents have higher C-SPAN than Real Rating assessments while eighteen presidents have lower ratings by C-SPAN than Real Ranking. There could be some political bias in these ratings, as C-SPAN ranks seventeen Democrats higher than does Real Ranking but only three are ranked lower, while with Republicans, C-SPAN ranks ten Republican presidents higher than does Real Ranking while rating fourteen Republican presidents lower than does Real Ranking. However, the C-SPAN ratings agree with the Real Ranking ratings to within 20% for twenty-one presidents: Washington, Lincoln, Reagan, John Adams, Polk, Nixon, Arthur, McKinley, Taft, Coolidge, Ford, Taylor, Hayes, Benjamin Harrison, Cleveland (twice), Fillmore, Garfield, Tyler, Van Buren, and Carter, while disagreeing by more than a factor of 2.0 (or 0.5) on only ten presidents. The second-worst discrepancy is with Andrew Jackson, who was given a 73.5 rating by C-SPAN but only a 20 rating by Real Ranking. Considering that Jackson ruined the economy of the country by his banking policies, and appointed probably the worst Supreme Court Chief Justice of all time, Roger B. Taney, it seems that the Real Ranking evaluation is the more valid of the two. The same can be said of the greatest discrepancy, regarding John F. Kennedy, where C-SPAN gave a rating of 79.4 while Real Ranking only accorded Kennedy a ten. Kennedy not only began the quagmire in Viet Nam by placing ground troops there, but he also gave the Soviets the excuse to build the Berlin Wall (and allowed them to do it), and his handling of the Cuban Missile Crisis resulted in NATO removing its missiles from Turkey. Both Jackson and Kennedy were extremely popular with the people at large, before, during, and after their presidencies, due to their successfully projected personas as "man of the people" and "super great guy," respectively. This further suggests that the more commonly published presidential ratings are based more on popularity contest criteria than on accomplishments. There appears to be an additional fault in the C-SPAN methodology; this can be noted by comparing the relative rankings of William Henry Harrison and Franklin Pierce. Leading strongly in the wrong direction, as exemplified by Franklin Pierce, produces a low C-SPAN rating, but providing no leadership, as in the case of William Henry Harrison, also produces a low rating. The methodology of the Real Ranking, which provides a 50 ranking for zero leadership, as in the case of William Henry Harrison, and a near zero rating for such poor leadership as provided by Franklin Pierce, is more consistent. Several non-controversial presidents who chose not to exercise leadership, with Real Ranking leadership ratings of 50, also have similar ratings from C-SPAN for crisis leadership. These include: Chester A. Arthur, Calvin Coolidge, James A. Garfield, Benjamin Harrison, and William Howard Taft.

Both systems provide a rating of 100 for most positive leadership; Abraham Lincoln has the highest rating from both, 100 (10 of 10) from Real Ranking and 97.8 by C-SPAN.

Other Rankings (data from Wikipedia: Historical rankings of the presidents of the United States)

Note: Professor Julian E. Zelizer of Princeton University says that traditional ratings are "weak mechanisms for evaluating."

Arthur Schlesinger, Sr. 1948, 1962
Arthur Schlesinger, Jr. 1996
Greatness in the White House: Rating the Presidents, from Washington Through Ronald Reagan by Robert K. Murray and Tim H. Blessing
Complete Book of U.S. Presidents 1982 survey by Chicago Tribune
Siena Research Institute of Siena College 1982, 1990, 1994, 2002, 2010
Rating the Presidents: A Ranking of U.S. Leaders from the Great and Honorable to the Dishonest and Incompetent by William J. Ridings, Jr. and Stuart B. McIver
C-SPAN 2000, 2009, 2017 (see page 160)

THE REAL RANKING OF THE PRESIDENTS

Wall Street Journal 2000 Survey

	PER ADJUSTED REAL RANKING	WALL STREET JOURNAL MINUS REAL RANKING
1	George Washington	0
2	Abraham Lincoln	0
3	Ronald Reagan	5
4	Thomas Jefferson	0
5	John Adams	8
6	James K. Polk	4
7	Theodore Roosevelt	-2
8	Dwight Eisenhower	1
9	Richard Nixon	24
10	George H.W. Bush	11
11	Chester A. Arthur	15
12	William McKinley	2
13	William Howard Taft	6
14	Herbert Hoover	15
15	Calvin Coolidge	10
16	Gerald Ford	12
17	James Monroe	-1
18	John Quincy Adams	2
19	Zachary Taylor	12
20	Rutherford B. Hays	2
21	Benjamin Harrison	6
22	Grover Cleveland	-10
23	U.S. Grant	9
24	Warren Harding	13
25	Millard Fillmore	10
26	Andrew Johnson	10
27	John Tyler	7
28	Martin Van Buren	-5
29	Jimmy Carter	1
30	Franklin Delano Roosevelt	-27
31	Harry Truman	-24
32	Bill Clinton	-8
33	John F. Kennedy	-15
34	James Madison	-19
35	Woodrow Wilson	-24
36	Lyndon Johnson	-19
37	Andrew Jackson	-31
38	James Buchanan	1
39	Franklin Pierce	-2
	William Henry Harrison	NOT RATED BY WALL STREET JOURNAL
	James A. Garfield	NOT RATED BY WALL STREET JOURNAL
	George W. Bush	NOT RATED BY WALL STREET JOURNAL
	Barrack Obama	NOT RATED BY WALL STREET JOURNAL
	Donald Trump	NOT RATED BY WALL STREET JOURNAL
	Grover Cleveland	ONLY RANKED ONCE BY WALL STREET JOURNAL

COMPARISON REAL RANKING vs WALL STREET JOURNAL, 2000
POSITIVE NUMBER = HIGHER RANKING BY REAL RANKING
NEGATIVE NUMBER = HIGHER RANKING BY WALL STREET JOURNAL
ZERO = EQUAL RANKING NUMBER

For the thirty-nine presidents rated by the Wall Street Journal, 13 presidents were ranked lower than the Real Ranking by WSJ and 23 were ranked higher. Only three presidents, George Washington, Abraham Lincoln, and Thomas Jefferson, had the same ranking from both surveys. For Democrats, WSJ ranked 12 higher than did RR. For Republicans, WSJ only ranked one, Theodore Roosevelt, higher than did RR. Fifteen presidents were ranked by WSJ within 5 points of their RR ranking. Only five presidents had rankings by WSJ that varied by 20 or more points from the RR ranking; four are Democrats: Franklin Roosevelt, Andrew Jackson, Harry Truman, and Woodrow Wilson, and one Republican, Richard Nixon.

Wall Street Journal 2005 for Federalist Society by James Lindgren of Northwestern University Law School
Times of London 2008 ranked 42 presidents
University of London, Iwan Morgan, United States Presidency Centre 2011
American Political Science Association 2015, 2018 (see *Newsweek*/APSA page 147)

The Wikipedia website provides an aggregate ranking for all the presidents based on all the rankings they included, a total of nineteen – some are updates of earlier rankings also included in the Wikipedia evaluation. Some of the surveys making up the aggregate exclude more recent presidents because they were performed prior to that president tasking office or completing his term. Nevertheless, comparing this aggregate or composite mainstream ranking with the Real Ranking can be informative:

Real Ranking (adjusted)	President (# of mainstream rankings)	Aggregate Ranking	Aggregate vs RR
1	Washington (19)	3	-2
2	Lincoln (19)	1	1
3	Reagan (15)	16	-13
4	Jefferson (19)	5	-1
5	John Adams (19)	15	-10
6	Polk (19)	12	-6
7	Theodore Roosevelt (19)	4	3
8	Eisenhower (18)	8	0
9	Nixon (17)	33	-24
10	George H.W. Bush (14)	22	-12
11	Arthur (19)	28	-17
12	McKinley (19)	19	-7
13	Taft (19)	23	-10
14	Hoover (19)	34	-20
15	Coolidge (19)	30	-15
16	Ford (17)	26	-10
17	Monroe (19)	17	0
18	John Quincy Adams (19)	21	-3
19	Taylor (19)	35	-16
20	Hayes (19)	25	-5
21	Benjamin Harrison (19)	31	-10
22	Garfield (11)	29	-7
23	Trump (1)	44 (only rated by 1)	-21
24	William H. Harrison (11)	38	-14
25 (comb)	Cleveland 1st, 2nd comb (19)	20	5
26	George W. Bush (8)	32	-6
27	Grant (19)	36	-9
28	Harding (19)	42	-14
29	Fillmore (19)	39	-10
30	Andrew Johnson (19)	41	-11
31	Tyler (19)	37	-6
32	Van Buren (19)	24	8
33	Carter (17)	27	6
34	Franklin D. Roosevelt (19)	2	32
35	Truman (18)	6	29
36	Clinton (13)	18	18
37	Kennedy (17)	10	27
38	Madison (19)	14	24
39	Wilson (19)	7	32
40	Obama (4)	11	29
41	Lyndon Johnson (17)	13	28
42	Jackson (19)	9	33
43	Buchanan (19)	43	0
44	Pierce (19)	40	4

The aggregate ranking is the same as the Real Ranking for three presidents: Monroe, Buchanan, and Eisenhower. The aggregate ranking is within 5 points of the Real Ranking for eleven presidents and differs by twenty points or more for eleven presidents. Of these, the Real Ranking ranks eight Democrats lower by twenty points or more, and ranks three Republicans higher. Real Ranking placed four Democrats higher than the aggregate: Jefferson, Tyler, Polk, and Andrew Johnson. Real Ranking ranked two Republicans lower than the aggregate: Lincoln and Theodore Roosevelt.

For the thirty presidents that were ranked by all nineteen rating systems, from Washington to Franklin Roosevelt and excluding William Henry Harrison and James A. Garfield who were rated by only eleven entities, Lincoln averaged the highest ranking, followed by Franklin Roosevelt, Washington, Theodore Roosevelt, Jefferson, Wilson, Jackson, Polk, Madison, John Adams, Monroe, McKinley, Cleveland, and John Quincy Adams, in order. The lowest average was for Buchanan, followed by Harding, Andrew Johnson, Pierce, Fillmore, Tyler, Grant, Taylor, Hoover, Benjamin Harrison, Coolidge, Arthur, Hayes, Van Buren, and Taft, in order. Not surprisingly, the four presidents leading up to the Civil War, all of whom failed to provide sufficient leadership to prevent it, are among the eight worst-rated presidents in this group per the aggregate.

The nineteen rankings tabulated by Wikipedia can be evaluated by looking at the range between lowest and highest rating for each president (rankings numbered from best = #1 to worst #44) :

THE REAL RANKING OF THE PRESIDENTS

President	Lowest Ranking	Highest Ranking	Range	Range Order (T = tie)
Washington	4	1	3	4
John Adams	19	9	10	12(T)
Jefferson	7	2	5	6(T)
Madison	20	6	14	24(T)
Monroe	18	6	12	17(T)
John Quincy Adams	25	11	14	24(T)
Jackson	18	5	13	20(T)
Van Buren	30	15	15	29(T)
William Henry Harrison*	42	26	16	32(T)
Tyler	39	22	17	36(T)
Polk	20	8	12	17(T)
Taylor	35	24	11	16
Fillmore	38	24	14	24(T)
Pierce	41	27	14	24(T)
Buchanan	43	26	17	36(T)
Lincoln	3	1	2	2(T)
Andrew Johnson	43	19	24	44
Grant	38	21	17	36(T)
Hayes	33	13	20	41(T)
Garfield*	34	25	9	10(T)
Arthur	35	17	18	40
Cleveland**	24	8	16	32(T)
Benjamin Harrison	34	19	15	29(T)
McKinley	21	11	10	12(T)
Theodore Roosevelt	7	2	5	6(T)
Taft	25	16	9	10(T)
Wilson	11	4	7	8
Harding	42	29	13	20(T)
Coolidge	36	23	13	20(T)
Hoover	36	19	17	36(T)
Franklin Delano Roosevelt	3	1	2	2(T)
Truman*	9	5	4	5
Eisenhower*	21	5	16	32(T)
Kennedy*	18	6	12	17(T)
Lyndon Johnson*	18	10	8	9
Nixon*	36	23	13	20(T)
Ford*	32	22	10	12(T)
Carter*	34	19	15	29(T)
Reagan*	26	6	20	41(T)
George H. W. Bush*	31	17	14	24(T)
Clinton*	24	8	16	32(T)
George W. Bush*	39	19	20	41(T)
Obama*	18	8	10	12(T)
Trump***	44	44	0	1

* Not all 19 rankings
** Combined Ranking
***Only ranked once

Not considering Trump, who was only ranked once, there is near consensus on 18 presidents, with ranking ranges of 12 or less; most of these presidents can be considered activists, who expanded the role of the presidency from its strict constitutional limits. On the contrary, only five presidents have rankings that vary by 18 or more; these were and remain controversial presidents. Interestingly, Republicans seem to improve more with time in the Wikipedia composite rankings; 19 Republican presidents improved over time in the rankings reported by Wikipedia, while only 13 Democrats did so. The number of presidents who declined in the rankings over time was equal, 5 Democrats and 5 Republicans. The greatest improvement was by six Republicans, with Grant up 19 points, Eisenhower up 16 points, Reagan up 14 points, Theodore Roosevelt up 14 points, Washington up 12 points, and Lincoln up 11 points. The best improvement by a Democrat was Truman, up 11 points (see Appendix F).

Ivan Eland "Recarving Rushmore" (2014) rated 41 presidents from the libertarian point of view: promoting prosperity, liberty, non-interventionism, and executive roles. A few conclusions from his evaluations: Washington: only one deserving to be on Mount Rushmore, Teddy Roosevelt: overrated, Lincoln: provoked civil war that did not achieve that much, Jefferson: was a hypocrite. Harding better, Truman worse than usually ranked.

There are noticeable differences in the Wikipedia composite ranking (referred to as "mainstream"), the Real Ranking, and the Eland (libertarian) ranking. As shown in Appendix D2, the Wikipedia composite favors strong presidents and dislikes moderate and weak ones, while Eland (libertarian) favors moderate and weak presidents and has a strong dislike for strong ones. Real Ranking has less partiality to strong or weak presidents than does the Wikipedia composite, while disagreeing with Eland on strong and weak presidents, and is neutral on moderate presidents. Reflecting its liberal bias, the Wikipedia composite mentions Eland, but does not include his ranking in its table of rankings.

The World Almanac and Book of Facts, in their 2019 edition, provide a ranking of the presidents, based on a survey of 91 "historians and other presidential observers"; C-SPAN's Historians Survey(s) on Presidential Leadership (and also data from C-SPAN's 2000 and 2009 surveys):

THE REAL RANKING OF THE PRESIDENTS

RANK, 2017	PRESIDENT	2009 RANK	2000 RANK
1	Lincoln	1	1
2	Washington	2	3
3	F.D. Roosevelt	3	2
4	T. Roosevelt	4	4
5	Eisenhower	8	9
6	Truman	5	6
7	Jefferson	7	7
8	Kennedy	6	8
9	Reagan	10	11
10	L. Johnson	11	10
11	Wilson	9	6
12	Obama	-	-
13	Monroe	14	14
14	Polk	12	12
15	Clinton	15	21
16	McKinley	16	15
17	Madison	20	18
18	Jackson	13	13
19	J. Adams	17	16
20	G.H.W. Bush	18	20
21	J.Q. Adams	19	19
22	Grant	23	33
23	Cleveland (only 1 rating)	21	17
24	Taft	24	24
25	Ford	22	23
26	Carter	25	22
27	Coolidge	26	27
28	Nixon	27	25
29	Garfield	28	29
30	B. Harrison	30	31
31	Taylor	29	28
32	Hayes	33	26
33	G.W. Bush	36	-
34	Van Buren	31	30
35	Arthur	32	32
36	Hoover	34	34
37	Fillmore	37	35
38	W.H. Harrison	39	37
39	Tyler	35	36
40	Harding	38	38
41	Pierce	40	39
42	A. Johnson	41	40
43	Buchanan	42	41

Trump was not included in the above ranking and Cleveland's two separate terms were combined.

As can be seen, the only presidents who have maintained a constant ranking in this latest composite, allowing for the timely inclusion of Obama and G.W. Bush, are Lincoln, Theodore Roosevelt, Jefferson, Pierce, Andrew Johnson, and Buchanan: Three universally ranked as among the best and three considered by nearly all to be among the worst. Among the others, some have increased in ranking in time, others have decreased, and a few seem to go up and down with the barometer. The greatest improvement was by U.S. Grant, who moved from 33rd to 22nd, 21st if the later addition to the rankings of Obama is discounted. The worst drop was by Cleveland and Hayes, both of whom were reduced by 6 slots, 5 without Obama, the same as Wilson. Appendix F elaborates on this.

What do the people say? From a Gallup poll conducted in 2011, asking 1,015 adults in the United States "Who (sic) do you regard as the greatest United States president?" Response was as follows:

Ronald Reagan	19%
Abraham Lincoln	14%
Bill Clinton	13%
John F. Kennedy	11%
George Washington	10%
Franklin Roosevelt	8%
Barrack Obama	5%
Theodore Roosevelt	3%
Harry Truman	3%
George W. Bush	2%
Thomas Jefferson	2%
Jimmy Carter	1%
Dwight Eisenhower	1%
George H. W. Bush	1%
Andrew Jackson	<0.5%
Lyndon B. Johnson	<0.5%
Richard Nixon	<0.5%

Personal memory is apparently a factor in popularity contests; only three of the presidents in the above list are from before the Civil War (there were a total of 15), while eleven are from after World War II (total 12 to 2011). The total is less than 94.5%; apparently 55 or so votes were scattered among other presidents. Eight of the top ten presidents per the Real Ranking are on the above list, as are nine of the top ten presidents from the average of the mainstream rankings compiled by Wikipedia, but only three of the libertarian top ten are on this list. Seven of the top ten per the APSA 2018 poll are in the top ten of this list, although not in the same order. The apparent flaws in public opinion polls are in evidence, only three presidents from the chronologically first fifteen are included; only two of the second fifteen, while twelve of the last fifteen and six of the most recent six presidents made the cut. The only president since the depression of the 1930s not on the list is Gerald Ford; he happens to be the only completely nonelected president (the poll was taken before Trump's presidency). Of the top ten listed, nine or ten can be considered popular personalities, both when they were president, and in retrospect.

The tendency over the last several decades has been for the United States' voting population to become increasingly conservative. The rate of increase in conservatism has increased up to the 2016 election. This may or may not continue. The liberal element of the population of the United States has grown increasingly frustrated, as evidenced by the extreme reaction against President Donald Trump. While the Constitutonal Amendment process appears to be closed to the liberal members of American society, due to the approval of 3/4 of the states requirement, a Constitutional Convention can be called, for the purpose of proposing amendments to the Constitution, with a vote of only 2/3 of the states. If such a convention were to be called, it would not necessarily be restricted to amendments, but could, conceivably, like the convention of 1787, completely replace the present Constitution with a new one. A more nationalistic framework of government, with greater reliance on popular vote and less emphasis on state sovereignty, particularly in the means of electing the president, could be the outcome.

APPENDIX A

REAL RANKING RATINGS FOR EACH PRESIDENT BASED ON FOUR CRITERIA

MAXIMUM RATING = 36

PRESIDENT	RANKING	MAKE AMERICA GREAT		IMPROVE QUALITY OF LIFE		MEET CRISES		OVERCOME OPPOSITION		TOTAL RATING
		VALUE	PCT	VALUE	PCT	VALUE	PCT	VALUE	PCT	
Washington	1	10	90%	8	80%	10	90%	8	50%	28.4
Lincoln	2	10	90%	8	55%	10	100%	8	60%	28.2
Reagan	3	10	80%	8	80%	10	80%	8	60%	27.2
Jefferson	4	10	100%	8	70%	10	60%	8	50%	25.6
J Adams	5	10	70%	8	70%	10	70%	8	70%	25.2
Polk	6	10	90%	8	60%	10	70%	8	50%	24.8
T Roosevelt	7	10	80%	8	80%	10	60%	8	50%	24.4
Eisenhower	8	10	70%	8	80%	10	60%	8	50%	23.4
Nixon	9	10	70%	8	80%	10	50%	8	60%	23.2
G H W Bush	10	10	65%	8	60%	10	60%	8	60%	22.1
Arthur	11	10	70%	8	55%	10	50%	8	70%	22.0
McKinley	12	10	70%	8	65%	10	55%	8	50%	21.7
Taft	13	10	75%	8	70%	10	50%	8	40%	21.3
Hoover	14	10	50%	8	35%	10	75%	8	70%	20.9
Coolidge	15	10	70%	8	70%	10	50%	8	40%	20.8
Ford	16	10	65%	8	65%	10	55%	8	40%	20.4
Monroe	17	10	60%	8	65%	10	50%	8	50%	20.2
J Q Adams	18	10	50%	8	65%	10	50%	8	50%	19.2
Taylor	19	10	60%	8	60%	10	50%	8	40%	19.0
Hayes	20	10	50%	8	50%	10	50%	8	60%	18.8
B Harrison	21	10	50%	8	50%	10	50%	8	50%	18.0
Garfield	22	10	50%	8	50%	10	50%	8	50%	18.0
Trump	23	10	50%	8	50%	10	50%	8	50%	18.0
W H Harrison	24	10	50%	8	50%	10	50%	8	50%	18.0
Cleveland(1)	25	10	40%	8	40%	10	60%	8	60%	18.0
Cleveland(2)	26	10	40%	8	35%	10	60%	8	60%	17.6
G W Bush	27	10	50%	8	50%	10	40%	8	50%	17.0
Grant	28	10	50%	8	50%	10	40%	8	50%	17.0
Harding	29	10	60%	8	60%	10	20%	8	50%	16.8
Fillmore	30	10	50%	8	50%	10	45%	8	40%	16.7
A Johnson	31	10	50%	8	50%	10	10%	8	75%	16.0
Tyler	32	10	40%	8	45%	10	40%	8	40%	14.8
Van Buren	33	10	40%	8	35%	10	40%	8	40%	14.0
Carter	34	10	40%	8	35%	10	35%	8	45%	13.9
F D Roosevelt	35	10	30%	8	30%	10	45%	8	45%	13.5
Truman	36	10	40%	8	25%	10	35%	8	45%	13.1
Clinton	37	10	30%	8	30%	10	25%	8	50%	11.9
Kennedy	38	10	30%	8	40%	10	10%	8	35%	10.0
Madison	39	10	25%	8	40%	10	10%	8	40%	9.9
Wilson	40	10	25%	8	25%	10	40%	8	15%	9.7
Obama	41	10	10%	8	20%	10	30%	8	40%	8.8
L Johnson	42	10	20%	8	30%	10	10%	8	30%	7.8
Jackson	43	10	30%	8	30%	10	20%	8	10%	7.0
Buchanan	44	10	25%	8	5%	10	20%	8	20%	6.5
Pierce	45	10	20%	8	10%	10	10%	8	*15%*	5.0

AVERAGE RATING   17.64

APPENDIX B PAGE 1

POPULAR VOTE FOR PRESIDENT 1788-2016

YEAR	WINNER	VOTE	PERCENT	LOSER(S) (max 4 highest)	TOTAL VOTE	
1788	Washington	69	100.0%	J Adams	69	ELECTORAL VOTE
1792	Washington	132	100.0%	J Adams, G Clinton	132	ELECTORAL VOTE
1796	J Adams	71	51.1%	Jefferson	139	ELECTORAL VOTE
1800	Jefferson	73	50.0%	Burr, J Adams, Pinckney	146	ELECTORAL VOTE
1804	Jefferson	162	92.0%	Pinckney	176	ELECTORAL VOTE
1808	Madison	122	72.2%	Pinckney, G Clinton	169	ELECTORAL VOTE
1812	Madison	128	59.0%	D W Clinton	217	ELECTORAL VOTE
1816	Monroe	183	84.3%	King	217	ELECTORAL VOTE
1820	Monroe	231	99.6%	J Q Adams	232	ELECTORAL VOTE
1824	J Q Adams	113,122	31.8%	Jackson, Crawford, Clay	355,242	POPULAR VOTE
1828	Jackson	647,231	56.0%	J Q Adams	1,156,328	POPULAR VOTE
1832	Jackson	687,502	56.5%	Clay, Floyd, Wirt	1,217,691	POPULAR VOTE
1836	Van Buren	762,678	58.2%	W H Harrison, White, Webster	1,310,685	POPULAR VOTE
1840	W H Harrisn	1,275,017	53.1%	Van Buren, Birney	2,403,089	POPULAR VOTE
1844	Polk	1,337,243	50.7%	Clay, Birney	2,636,311	POPULAR VOTE
1848	Taylor	1,361,393	47.3%	Cass, Van Buren	2,876,354	POPULAR VOTE
1852	Pierce	1,601,474	53.6%	Scott, Hale	2,988,052	POPULAR VOTE
1856	Buchanan	1,836,072	45.3%	Fremont, Fillmore	4,051,480	POPULAR VOTE
1860	Lincoln	1,865,908	45.0%	Douglas, Breckinridge, Bell	4,149,271	POPULAR VOTE
1864	Lincoln	2,216,066	55.1%	McClellan	4,024,791	POPULAR VOTE
1868	Grant	3,015,071	52.7%	Seymour	5,724,686	POPULAR VOTE
1872	Grant	3,597,070	55.9%	Greeley	6,431,149	POPULAR VOTE
1876	Hayes	4,034,311	48.5%	Tilden	8,322,857	POPULAR VOTE
1880	Garfield	4,449,053	50.0%	Hancock	8,891,683	POPULAR VOTE
1884	Cleveland	4,911,017	50.3%	Blaine	9,759,351	POPULAR VOTE
1888	B Harrison	5,443,892	49.6%	Cleveland	10,978,380	POPULAR VOTE
1892	Cleveland	5,551,883	47.2%	B Harrison, Weaver	11,758,456	POPULAR VOTE
1896	McKinley	7,035,638	52.1%	Bryan	13,503,584	POPULAR VOTE
1900	McKinley	7,219,530	53.2%	Bryan	13,577,601	POPULAR VOTE
1904	T Roosevelt	7,828,834	60.6%	Parker, Debs	12,913,325	POPULAR VOTE
1908	Taft	7,679,005	54.5%	Bryan, Debs	14,088,111	POPULAR VOTE
1912	Wilson	6,293,152	45.3%	Taft, T Roosevelt, Debs	13,896,281	POPULAR VOTE
1916	Wilson	9,129,606	51.7%	Hughes, Benson	17,667,827	POPULAR VOTE
1920	Harding	16,152,200	63.8%	Cox, Debs	25,299,553	POPULAR VOTE
1924	Coolidge	15,725,018	54.3%	Davis, La Follette	28,933,460	POPULAR VOTE
1928	Hoover	21,392,190	58.8%	Smith, Thomas	36,408,632	POPULAR VOTE
1932	F D Roosevel	54,281,858	59.2%	Hoover, Thomas	91,739,076	POPULAR VOTE
1936	F D Roosevel	27,751,597	62.5%	Landon, Lemke	44,431,180	POPULAR VOTE
1940	F D Roosevel	27,243,466	55.0%	Wilkie	49,548,221	POPULAR VOTE
1944	F D Roosevel	25,602,505	53.8%	Dewey	47,608,783	POPULAR VOTE
1948	Truman	24,179,345	49.9%	Dewey, Thurmond, H A Wallace	48,496,829	POPULAR VOTE
1952	Eisenhower	33,938,252	55.4%	Stevenson	61,253,244	POPULAR VOTE
1956	Eisenhower	35,585,316	57.8%	Stevenson	61,616,638	POPULAR VOTE
1960	Kennedy	34,227,096	50.1%	Nixon, Byrd	68,333,642	POPULAR VOTE
1964	L Johnson	43,126,506	61.3%	Goldwater	70,303,305	POPULAR VOTE
1968	Nixon	31,785,480	43.6%	Humphrey, George C Wallace	72,967,119	POPULAR VOTE
1972	Nixon	47,165,234	61.8%	McGovern	76,336,008	POPULAR VOTE
1976	Carter	40,828,929	51.1%	Ford	79,977,869	POPULAR VOTE
1980	Reagan	43,899,246	51.6%	Carter, Anderson	85,100,118	POPULAR VOTE
1984	Reagan	54,281,858	59.2%	Mondale	91,739,076	POPULAR VOTE
1988	G H W Bush	48,881,921	53.9%	Dukakis	90,687,343	POPULAR VOTE
1992	W Clinton	44,908,254	43.3%	G H W Bush, Perot	103,751,662	POPULAR VOTE
1996	W Clinton	47,401,185	50.1%	Dole, Perot	94,683,948	POPULAR VOTE
2000	G W Bush	50,459,211	48.4%	Gore, Nader	104,297,515	POPULAR VOTE
2004	G W Bush	62,040,610	51.2%	Gore	121,069,054	POPULAR VOTE
2008	Obama	69,456,897	53.7%	McCain	129,391,711	POPULAR VOTE
2012	Obama	65,915,795	52.0%	Romney	126,849,299	POPULAR VOTE
2016	Trump	62,984,678	48.9%	H Clinton ONLY	128,838,327	POPULAR VOTE
2016	Trump	62,984,678	46.8%	H Clinton, Johnson, Stein, McMullin	134,635,321	POPULAR VOTE

APPENDIX B PAGE 2

RANKING	REAL RANKING	WIN VOTE	TOTAL VOTE	WINNER PERCENTAGE		
1	1	69	69	100.0%	WASHINGTON 1ST	
2	1	132	132	100.0%	WASHINGTON 2ND	
3	17	231	232	99.6%	MONROE 2ND	
4	4	162	176	92.0%	JEFFERSON 2ND	
5	17	183	217	84.3%	MONROE 1ST	
6	39	122	169	72.2%	MADISON 1ST	
7	29	16,152,200	25,299,553	63.8%	HARDING	
8	35	27,751,597	44,431,180	62.5%	F D ROOSEVELT 2ND	
9	9	47,165,234	76,336,008	61.8%	NIXON 2ND	
10	42	43,126,506	70,303,305	61.3%	L JOHNSON	
11	7	7,828,834	12,913,325	60.6%	T ROOSEVELT	
12	3	54,281,858	91,739,076	59.2%	REAGAN 2ND	
13	35	22,821,857	38,583,698	59.1%	F D ROOSEVELT 1ST	
14	39	128	217	59.0%	MADISON'S 2ND	
15	14	21,392,190	36,408,632	58.8%	HOOVER	
16	33	762,678	1,310,685	58.2%	VAN BUREN	
17	8	35,585,316	61,616,638	57.8%	EISENHOWER 2ND	
18	43	687,502	1,217,691	56.5%	JACKSON 2ND	
19	43	647,231	1,156,328	56.0%	JACKSON 1ST	
20	28	3,597,070	6,431,149	55.9%	GRANT 2ND	
21	8	33,938,252	61,253,244	55.4%	EISENHOWER 1ST	
22	2	2,216,066	4,024,791	55.1%	LINCOLN 2	
23	35	27,243,466	49,548,221	55.0%	F D ROOSEVELT 3RD	
24	13	7,679,005	14,088,111	54.5%	TAFT	
25	15	15,725,018	28,933,460	54.3%	COOLIDGE	3-man race
26	10	48,881,921	90,687,343	53.9%	G H W BUSH	
27	35	25,602,505	47,608,783	53.8%	F D ROOSEVELT 4TH	
28	41	69,456,897	129,391,711	53.7%	OBAMA 1ST	
29	45	1,601,474	2,988,052	53.6%	PIERCE	
30	12	7,219,530	13,577,601	53.2%	MCKINLEY 2ND	
31	24	1,275,017	2,403,089	53.1%	W H HARRISON	
32	28	3,015,071	5,724,686	52.7%	GRANT 1ST	
33	12	7,035,638	13,503,584	52.1%	MCKINLEY 1ST	
34	41	65,915,795	126,849,299	52.0%	OBAMA 2ND	
35	40	9,129,606	17,667,827	51.7%	WILSON 2ND	
36	3	43,899,246	85,100,118	51.6%	REAGAN 1ST	includes J Anderson vote
37	27	62,040,610	121,069,054	51.2%	G W BUSH 2ND	
38	5	71	139	51.079%	J ADAMS	
39	34	40,828,929	79,977,869	51.050%	CARTER	
40	6	1,337,243	2,636,311	50.7%	POLK	
41	25	4,911,017	9,759,351	50.3%	CLEVELAND 1ST	
42	38	34,227,096	68,333,642	50.1%	KENNEDY	
43	37	47,401,185	94,683,948	50.1%	CLINTON 2ND	3 man race
44	22	4,449,053	8,891,683	50.036%	GARFIELD	
45	4	73	146	50.0%	JEFFERSON 1ST	
46	36	24,179,345	48,496,829	49.9%	TRUMAN	
47	21	5,443,892	10,978,380	49.6%	B HARRISON	
48	23	62,984,678	134,635,321	48.9%	TRUMP-CLINTON ONLY	TOTAL VOTE 134,635,321
49	20	4,034,311	8,322,857	48.5%	HAYES	
50	27	50,459,211	104,297,515	48.4%	G W BUSH 1ST	
51	19	1,361,393	2,876,354	47.3%	TAYLOR	3-man race
52	26	5,551,883	11,758,456	47.2%	CLEVELAND 2ND	3 man race
53	44	1,836,072	4,051,480	45.319%	BUCHANAN	3-man race
54	40	6,293,152	13,896,281	45.287%	WILSON 1ST	Wilson vs Taft vs T Roosevelt
55	2	1,865,908	4,149,271	45.0%	LINCOLN 1ST	4 man race
56	9	31,785,480	72,967,119	43.6%	NIXON 1ST	3-man race
57	37	44,908,254	103,751,662	43.3%	CLINTON 1ST	3 man race
58	18	113,122	355,242	31.8%	J Q ADAMS	4-man race
	11	NO ELECTION			(ARTHUR)	
	16	LOST ATTEMPT TO RETAIN PRESIDENCY			(FORD)	
	30	NO ELECTION EXCEPT LATER 3RD PARTY			(FILLMORE)	
	31	NO ELECTION			(A JOHNSON)	
	32	NO ELECTION			(TYLER)	

APPENDIX C PAGE 1

PRESIDENTS AND CONGRESS 1789-1925

CONTROL OF THE GOVERNMENT - PRESIDENTS AND CONGRESS 1789-2019   PARTY: R=REPUBLICAN, WHIG, FEDERALIST, WASHINGTON
M=MIXED
D=DEMOCRAT, ANTIFEDERALIST, DEMOCRATIC REPUBLICAN, "REPUBLICAN", JACKSONIAN

CONGRESS HOUSE PARTY OF SPEAKER	DATE START	SENATE MAJORITY LEADER - OFFICIAL - 1919	CONGRESS	PRESIDENT	GOVT
1 WASH	1789	WASH	R	WASHINGTON	R
2 F	1791	AF, F	M	WASHINGTON	M
3 AF	1793	F, AF	M	WASHINGTON	M
4 F	1795	DR, F	M	WASHINGTON	M
5 F	1797	F	R	J ADAMS	R
6 F	1799	F	R	J ADAMS	R
7 DR	1801	"REP"	D	JEFFERSON	D
8 DR	1803	"REP"	D	JEFFERSON	D
9 DR	1805	"REP"	D	JEFFERSON	D
10 DR	1807	"REP"	D	JEFFERSON	D
11 DR	1809	"REP"	D	MADISON	D
12 DR	1811	"REP"	D	MADISON	D
13 DR	1813	"REP"	D	MADISON	D
14 DR	1815	"REP"	D	MADISON	D
15 DR	1817	"REP"	D	MONROE	D
16 DR	1819	"REP"	D	MONROE	D
17 "REP"	1821	"REP"	D	MONROE	D
18 DR	1823	"REP"	D	MONROE	D
19 "REP"	1825	JACK	D	JQ ADAMS	M
20 JACK	1827	JACK	D	JQ ADAMS	M
21 JACK	1829	JACK	D	JACKSON	D
22 JACK	1831	JACK	D	JACKSON	D
23 JACK	1833	JACK	D	JACKSON	D
24 DEM	1835	JACK	D	JACKSON	D
25 DEM	1837	DEM	D	VAN BUREN	D
26 DEM	1839	DEM	D	VAN BUREN	D
27 WHIG	1841	DEM-WHIG	M	W H HARRISON	M
28 DEM	1843	WHIG	M	TYLER	M
29 DEM	1845	DEM	D	POLK	D
30 WHIG	1847	DEM	M	POLK	M
31 DEM	1849	DEM	D	TAYLOR	M
32 DEM	1851	DEM	D	FILLMORE	M
33 DEM	1853	DEM	D	PIERCE	D
34 AMER	1855	DEM	M	PIERCE	M
35 DEM	1857	DEM	D	BUCHANAN	D
36 REP	1859	DEM-REP	M	BUCHANAN	M
37 REP	1861	REP	R	LINCOLN	R
38 REP	1863	REP	R	LINCOLN	R
39 REP	1865	REP	R	LINCOLN	R
40 REP	1867	REP	R	A JOHNSON	M
41 REP	1869	REP	R	GRANT	R
42 REP	1871	REP	R	GRANT	R
43 REP	1873	REP	R	GRANT	R
44 DEM	1875	REP	M	GRANT	M
45 DEM	1877	REP	M	HAYES	M
46 DEM	1879	DEM	D	HAYES	M
47 REP	1881	DEM-IND-REP	M	GARFIELD	M
48 DEM	1883	REP	M	ARTHUR	M
49 DEM	1885	REP	M	CLEVELAND	M
50 DEM	1887	REP	M	CLEVELAND	M
51 REP	1889	REP	R	B HARRISON	R
52 DEM	1891	REP	M	B HARRISON	M
53 DEM	1893	REP-DEM	M	CLEVELAND	M
54 REP	1895	REP	R	CLEVELAND	M
55 REP	1897	REP	R	MCKINLEY	R
56 REP	1899	REP	R	MCKINLEY	R
57 REP	1901	REP	R	MCKINLEY	R
58 REP	1903	REP	R	T ROOSEVELT	R
59 REP	1905	REP	R	T ROOSEVELT	R
60 REP	1907	REP	R	T ROOSEVELT	R
61 REP	1909	REP	R	TAFT	R
62 DEM	1911	REP-DEM	M	TAFT	M
63 DEM	1913	DEM	D	WILSON	D
64 DEM	1915	DEM	D	WILSON	D
65 DEM	1917	DEM	D	WILSON	D
66 REP	1919	REP	R	WILSON	M
67 REP	1921	REP	R	HARDING	R
68 REP	1923	REP	R	HARDNG	R
69 REP	1925	REP	R	COOLIDGE	R

GOVERNMENT
FROM 1789 THROUGH 1799

REP	3	50.0%
MIX	3	50.0%
DEM	0	0.0%

PRESIDENT

REP	6	100.0%
MIX	0	0.0%
DEM	0	0.0%

LONGEST STRETCH

"REPUBLICAN' I E DEMOCRAT
FROM 1801 TO 1825 = 24 YEARS

IF J Q ADAMS CONSIDERED "REPUBLICAN"
FROM 1801-1841 = 40 YEARS

GOVERNMENT
FROM 1801 THROUGH 1859

REP	0	0.0%
MIX	9	30.0%
DEM	21	70.0%

PRESIDENT

REP	5	16.7%
MIX	1	3.3%
DEM	24	80.0%

GOVERNMENT
FROM 1861 TROUGH 1929

REP	19	54.3%
MIX	13	37.1%
DEM	3	8.6%

PRESIDENT

REP	26	74.3%
MIX	1	2.9%
DEM	8	22.9%

NO MORE MIDTERM CHANGE
APRIL 8 1913 17TH AMENDMENT
DIRECT ELECTION OF SENATORS

APPENDIX C PAGE 2

PRESIDENTS AND CONGRESS 1927-2020

PARTY: R=REPUBLICAN, WHIG, FEDERALIST, WASHINGTON
M=MIXED
D=DEMOCRAT, ANTIFEDERALIST, DEMOCRATIC REPUBLICAN, "REPUBLICAN", JACKSONIAN

CONTROL OF THE GOVERNMENT - PRESIDENTS AND CONGRESS 1789-2019

CONGRESS	HOUSE PARTY OF SPEAKER	DATE START	SENATE MAJORITY LEADER - OFFICIAL - 1919	CONGRESS	PRESIDENT	GOVT			
70	REP	1927	REP	R	COOLIDGE	R			
71	REP	1929	REP	R	HOOVER	R			
72	DEM	1931	REP	M	HOOVER	M			
73	DEM	1933	DEM	D	F D ROOSEVELT	D			
74	DEM	1935	DEM	D	F D ROOSEVELT	D			
75	DEM	1937	DEM	D	F D ROOSEVELT	D			
76	DEM	1939	DEM	D	F D ROOSEVELT	D			
77	DEM	1941	DEM	D	F D ROOSEVELT	D			
78	DEM	1943	DEM	D	F D ROOSEVELT	D			
79	DEM	1945	DEM	D	F D ROOSEVELT	D			
80	REP	1947	REP	R	TRUMAN	M			
81	DEM	1949	DEM	D	TRUMAN	D			
82	DEM	1951	DEM	D	TRUMAN	D			
83	REP	1953	REP	R	EISENHOWER	R	GOVERNMENT		
84	DEM	1955	DEM	D	EISENHOWER	M	FROM 1931 THROUGH 1979		
85	DEM	1957	DEM	D	EISENHOWER	M			
86	DEM	1959	DEM	D	EISENHOWER	M	REP	1	4.0%
87	DEM	1961	DEM	D	KENNEDY	D	MIX	9	36.0%
88	DEM	1963	DEM	D	KENNEDY	D	DEM	15	60.0%
89	DEM	1965	DEM	D	L JOHNSON	D			
90	DEM	1967	DEM	D	L JOHNSON	D	PRESIDENT		
91	DEM	1969	DEM	D	NIXON	M			
92	DEM	1971	DEM	D	NIXON	M	REP	9	36.0%
93	DEM	1973	DEM	D	NIXON	M	MIX	0	0.0%
94	DEM	1975	DEM	D	FORD	M	DEM	16	64.0%
95	DEM	1977	DEM	D	CARTER	D			
96	DEM	1979	DEM	D	CARTER	D			
97	DEM	1981	REP	M	REAGAN	M			
98	DEM	1983	REP	M	REAGAN	M	GOVERNMENT		
99	DEM	1985	REP	M	REAGAN	M	FROM 1981 THROUGH 2020		
100	DEM	1987	DEM	D	REAGAN	M			
101	DEM	1989	DEM	D	GHW BUSH	M	REP	3	15.0%
102	DEM	1991	DEM	D	GHW BUSH	M	MIX	15	75.0%
103	DEM	1993	DEM	D	CLINTON	D	DEM	2	10.0%
104	REP	1995	REP	R	CLINTON	M			
105	REP	1997	REP	R	CLINTON	M	PRESIDENT		
106	REP	1999	REP	R	CLINTON	M			
107	REP	2001	DEM	M	GW BUSH	M	REP	12	60.0%
108	REP	2003	REP	R	GW BUSH	R	MIX	0	0.0%
109	REP	2005	REP	R	GW BUSH	R	DEM	8	40.0%
110	DEM	2007	DEM	D	GW BUSH	M			
111	DEM	2009	DEM	D	OBAMA	D			
112	REP	2011	DEM	M	OBAMA	M			
113	REP	2013	DEM	M	OBAMA	M			
114	REP	2015	REP	R	OBAMA	M			
115	REP	2017	REP	R	TRUMP	R			
116	DEM	2019	REP	M	TRUMP	M			

TOTAL 1789-2019	HOUSE	SENATE		CONGRESS			PRESIDENT			GOVERNMENT	
REP	44	46	REP	34	29.31%		REP	58	50.00%	26	22.41%
MIX	0	8	MIX	25	21.55%		MIX	2	1.72%	49	42.24%
DEM	72	62	DEM	57	49.14%		DEM	56	48.28%	41	35.34%
TOTALSINCE 1980			REP	7	35.00%		REP	12	60.00%	3	15.00%
REP	10	11	MIX	7	35.00%		MIX	0	0.00%	15	75.00%
DEM	10	9	DEM	6	30.00%		DEM	8	40.00%	2	10.00%

TOTALS			REP	29.3%	REP	22.4%
REP	44		MIX	21.6%	MIX	42.2%
DEM	72		DEM	49.1%	DEM	35.3%
TOTALSINCE 1980			REP	170.0%	REP	130.0%
REP	10		MIX	125.0%	MIX	240.0%
DEM	10		DEM	285.0%	DEM	210.0%

HTTPS://WWW.SENATE.GOV/ARTANDHISTORY/HISTORY/RESOURCES/PDF/CHRONLIST.PDF

APPENDIX D1

COMPARISON OF REAL RANKINGS WITH MAINSTREAM AND LIBERTARIAN RANKINGS

REAL RANKINGS FOR EACH PRESIDENT- COMPARED TO OTHER SYSTEMS: LIBERTARIAN PER ELAND, 19 MAINSTREAM RANKINGS (SEE TEXT)

PRESIDENT	REAL RANKING	LIBERTARIAN ELAND	MAINSTREAM HIGH	MAINSTREAM LOW	RANGE RR-LIBERT	RANGE H-L MAINSTR	INSIDE MAINSTREAM RR	INSIDE MAINSTREAM LIBERTARIAN	IN MAIN TO WITHIN 5 RR	IN MAIN TO WITHIN 5 LIBERTARIAN	+20 TO MAINSTREAM RR	+20 TO MAINSTREAM LIBERTARIAN
washington	1	7	1	4	6	3	Y	N	Y	Y		
lincoln	2	29	1	3	27	2	Y	N	Y	N		Y
reagan	3	35	6	26	32	20	N	N	Y	N		
jefferson	4	26	2	7	22	5	Y	N	Y	N		
J adams	5	22	9	19	17	10	N	N	Y	Y		
polk	6	38	9	20	32	11	N	N	Y	N		
troosevelt	7	21	2	7	14	5	N	N	Y	N		
eisenhower	8	9	5	21	1	16	Y	Y	Y	Y		
nixon	9	30	23	36	21	13	N	Y	N	Y		
ghwbush	10	33	17	31	23	14	N	N	N	Y		
arthur	11	5	17	35	6	18	N	N	N	N		
mckinley	12	39	11	21	27	10	Y	N	Y	N		
taft	13	20	16	25	7	9	N	Y	Y	Y		
hoover	14	18	19	38	4	19	N	N	Y	Y		
coolidge	15	10	23	36	5	13	N	N	N	N		
ford	16	16	23	32	0	9	N	N	N	N		
monroe	17	25	7	18	8	11	Y	N	Y	N		
j q adams	18	12	11	25	6	14	Y	Y	Y	Y		
taylor	19	13	24	35	6	11	N	N	Y	N		
hayes	20	4	13	33	16	20	Y	N	Y	N		
bharrison	21	15	19	34	6	15	Y	N	Y	Y		
garfield	22	NR		25	34	XX	9	N	XX	Y	XX		XX
trump	23	NR		44	44	XX	0	N	XX	N	XX	Y	XX
w h harrison	24	NR		26	42	XX	16	N	XX	Y	XX		XX
cleveland (1)	25	2	8	24	23	16	N	N	Y	N		
cleveland (2)	26	2	8	24	24	16	N	N	Y	N		
g w vbush	27	37	19	39	10	20	Y	Y	Y	Y		
grant	28	19	21	38	9	17	Y	N	Y	Y		
harding	29	6	29	42	23	13	Y	N	Y	N		Y
fillmore	30	14	24	38	16	14	Y	N	Y	N		
a johnson	31	17	19	42	14	23	Y	N	Y	Y		
tyler	32	1	22	39	31	17	Y	N	Y	N		Y
van buren	33	3	15	34	30	19	Y	N	Y	N		
carter	34	8	18	34	26	16	Y	N	Y	N		
f d roosevelt	35	31	1	3	4	2	N	N	N	N	Y	Y
truman	36	40	5	9	4	4	N	N	N	N	Y	Y
clinton	37	11	8	24	26	16	N	Y	N	Y		
kennedy	38	36	8	16	2	8	N	N	N	N	Y	Y
madison	39	28	8	20	11	12	N	N	N	N		
wilson	40	41	4	11	1	7	N	N	N	N	Y	Y
obama	41	34	8	18	7	10	N	N	N	N	Y	
l johnson	42	32	10	17	10	7	N	N	N	N	Y	
jackson	43	27	5	18	16	13	N	N	N	N	Y	
buchanan	44	23	26	43	21	17	N	N	Y	Y		
pierce	45	24	27	41	21	14	N	N	Y	Y		
YES TOTAL							17	6	30	15	8	7
NO TOTAL							28	36	15	27		

APPENDIX D2

WEAK, MODERATE, AND STRONG PRESIDENTS

rankings adjusted for W H Harrison, Garfield, and Cleveland to compare to mainstream rankings

PRESIDENT	WEAK	MOD	STRONG	WEAK PRESIDENTS RR RANK	WEAK PRESIDENTS LIB RANK	WEAK PRESIDENTS MAIN A R	MODERATE PRESIDENTS RR RANK	MODERATE PRESIDENTS LIB RANK	MODERATE PRESIDENTS MAIN AR	STRONG PRESIDENTS RR RANK	STRONG PRESIDENTS LIB RANK	STRONG PRESIDENTS MAIN A R	MAINSTR AVERAGE	LIB ADJ RANKING
Washington			Y							1	8	3	3	8
Lincoln			Y							2	33	1	1	33
Reagan			Y							3	39	16	16	39
Jefferson			Y							4	30	5	5	30
J Adams			Y							5	26	15	15	26
Polk			Y							6	42	12	12	42
T Roosevelt			Y							7	25	4	4	25
Eisenhower			Y							8	10	8	8	10
Nixon			Y							9	34	34	34	34
G H W Bush	Y			10	37	23							23	37
Arthur		Y					11	6	29				29	6
McKinley	Y			12	43	19							19	43
Taft		Y					13	24	24				24	24
Hoover		Y					14	22	35				35	22
Coolidge		Y					15	11	31				31	11
Ford	Y			16	20	27							27	20
Monroe		Y					17	29	17				17	29
J Q Adams		Y					18	13	22				22	13
Taylor		Y					19	14	36				36	14
Hayes		Y					20	5	26				26	5
B Harrison	Y			21	16	32							32	16
Garfield	Y			22	17	30							30	17
Trump			Y							23	18	45	45	18
W H Harrison	Y			24	19	39							39	19
Cleveland 1		Y					25	2	20				20	2
Cleveland 2		Y					26	2	20				20	2
G W Bush		Y					27	41	33				33	41
Grant	Y			28	23	37							37	23
Harding	Y			29	7	43							43	7
Fillmore	Y			30	15	40							40	15
A Johnson		Y					31	21	42				42	21
Tyler		Y					32	1	38				38	1
Van Buren	Y			33	4	25							25	4
Carter	Y			34	9	28							28	9
F D Roosevelt			Y							35	35	2	2	35
Truman			Y							36	44	6	6	44
Clinton	Y			37	12	18							18	12
Kennedy	Y			38	40	10							10	40
Madison	Y			39	32	14							14	32
Wilson			Y							40	45	7	7	45
Obama		Y					41	38	11				11	38
L Johnson			Y							42	36	13	13	36
Jackson			Y							43	31	9	9	31
Buchanan	Y			44	27	44							44	27
Pierce		Y					45	28	41				41	28
TOTAL	15	15	15	R RANK	I L RANK	MAIN R	R RANK	I L RANK	MAIN R	R RANK	I L RANK	MAIN R		
AVERAGES:				27.80	21.40	28.60	23.60	17.13	28.33	17.60	30.40	12.00		

NOTE: EQUAL PARTITION OF WEAK, MODERATE, STRONG PRESIDENTS IS PURELY COINCIDENCE

RR MEDIAN = 23 ALL OTHERS ADJUSTED TO MATCH

WEAK PRES ELAND LIBERT LIKES, MAINSTREAM DOES NOT   STRONG PRES MAINSTREAM LIKES ELAND LIBERT DOES NOT, A LITTLE

MAINSTREAM (WIKIPEDIA AVERAGE) LIKES STRONG DISLIKES WEAK AND MODERATE
LIBERTARIAN (I L) LIKES MODERATE, WEAK (A LITTLE) DISLIKES STRONG
REAL RANKING LIKES STRONG, NEUTRAL ON MODERATE, DISLIKES WEAK (A LITTLE)

FIRST 15 PRESIDENTS:	5 STRONG	5 MODERATE	5 WEAK
MIDDLE 15 PRESIDENTS	3	7	5
LATEST 15 PRESIDENTS	7	3	5

APPENDIX E PAGE 1

REAL RANKING COMPARED TO OTHER PRESIDENTIAL RANKINGS

# President	SCHLESINGER SR 1948	RR ADJU	DELTA RR VS SCH 48	SCHLESINGER 1962	RR ADJU	DELTA RR VS SCH 62	M-B 1982	RR ADJU	DELTA M-B VS RR	CHICAGO TRIBUNE 1982	RR ADJUS	DELTA CT 82 VS RR	SIENA 1982	RR ADJUS	DELTA SIENA 82 VS RR	SIENA 1990	RR ADJUS	DELTA SIENA 90 VS RR	SIENA 1994	RR ADJUS	DELTA SIENA 94 VS RR	RIDINGS & McIVER 1996	RR ADJUS	DELTA R&M 1996 VS RR	RANK SCHLESINGER 1996	SCORE '96 SCHLES	SHOULD BE	RR ADJU	DELTA SCHLES 96 VS RR	REAL RANKING FEB 5, 2019
1 WASHINGTON	1	1		1	1		3	1	2		1	1	4	1	3	4	1	3	4	1	3	3	1	2	2	3.97		1	1	1
2 ADAMS	4	5		4	6		9	4	5		4	11	8	5	3	14	5	9	12	5	7	14	5	9	11	2.32		5	6	5
3 JEFFERSON	3	2		3	2		4	3	1		3	2	3	4	1	3	4	1	5	4	1	4	4	0	4	3.38		4	0	4
4 MADISON	25	11		27	15		14	31	17		31	14	12	34	22	8	35	27	9	36	27	10	36	26	18	1.83		34	16	39
5 MONROE	12	0		13	5		15	15	0		15	1	16	16	0	11	17	6	15	17	2	13	17	4	16	2.15		17	1	17
6 J Q ADAMS	13	2		14	1		16	16	0		16	3	17	17	0	16	18	2	17	18	1	18	18	1	18	1.74		18	1	18
7 JACKSON	27	21		29	23		7	34	27		34	27	9	37	28	9	38	29	11	39	28	8	39	31	5	3.34		37	32	43
8 VAN BUREN	23	8		24	7		20	26	6		26	8	21	29	9	22	30	8	21	30	9	22	30	9	22	1.56		28	6	33
9 W H HARRISON	NR			NR			NR			NR			25	22	3	35	23	12	28	23	5	35	23	12	NR					24
10 TYLER	22	0		23	2		28	25	3		25	3	32	28	4	33	29	5	34	29	5	34	29	5	33	0.68		27	6	32
11 POLK	5	5		5	3		12	5	7		5	5	11	6	5	13	6	7	14	6	8	11	6	5	9	2.71		6	3	6
12 TAYLOR	14	11		15	9		27	17	10		17	9	31	18	13	34	19	15	33	19	14	29	19	10	30	0.88		19	11	19
13 FILLMORE	20	4		21	5		29	23	6		23	8	29	26	3	32	27	5	35	27	8	36	27	9	32	0.77		25	7	30
14 PIERCE	29	2		31	3		31	36	5		36	3	34	39	5	36	40	4	37	41	4	37	41	4	34	-9	-0.3333	39	5	45
15 BUCHANAN	28	2		30	1		33	35	2		35	0	38	39	1	39	40	1	40	40	0	40	40	0	39	-38	-1.3571	38	1	44
16 LINCOLN	2	1		2	1		1	2	1		2	1	1	2	1	2	2	0	2	2	0	1	2	1	1	4		2	1	2
17 A JOHNSON	21	2		22	1		32	24	8		24	6	36	27	9	39	28	11	40	28	12	39	28	11	38	-23	-0.8846	26	12	31
18 GRANT	18	10		19	11		35	21	14		21	11	37	25	13	37	25	13	38	25	13	38	25	13	40	-9	-1	23	12	28
19 HAYES	15	2		16	2		22	18	4		18	4	26	19	7	23	20	3	24	20	4	25	20	5	24	-9	1.48	20	4	20
20 GARFIELD	NR			NR			NR			NR			23	21	2	30	22	8	26	22	4	30	22	8	NR					22
21 ARTHUR	7	10		8	13		23	9	14		9	15	22	10	12	26	11	16	28	11	17	27	11	17	27	1.4		11	16	11
22 CLEVELAND 1	17	9		18	7		17	20	3		20	7	15	23	8	17	24	7	19	24	5	16	24	8	13	2.24		22	9	25
23 B HARRISON	16	5		17	3		26	19	7		19	6	28	20	8	29	21	8	30	21	9	31	21	10	20	1.67		21	1	21
24 CLEVELAND 2	17	9		18	7		17	20	3		20	7	15	23	8	17	24	7	19	24	5	16	24	8	13	2.24		22	9	26
25 MCKINLEY	8	10		9	6		18	10	8		10	1	18	11	7	19	12	7	18	12	6	17	12	5	17	2.11		12	5	12
26 T ROOSEVELT	6	1		6	1		5	6	1		6	2	5	7	2	5	7	2	3	7	4	5	7	2	6	3.31		7	1	7
27 TAFT	9	7		10	6		19	11	8		11	9	19	12	7	20	13	8	21	13	8	20	13	7	23	1.52		13	10	13
28 WILSON	26	22		28	24		6	32	26		32	26	6	35	29	6	36	30	6	37	31	6	37	31	7	3.21		35	28	40
29 HARDING	19	10		20	11		36	22	14		22	14	39	25	14	40	26	14	41	26	15	41	26	15	40	-48	-1.7143	24	16	29
30 COOLIDGE	11	12		12	15		30	13	17		13	16	33	14	19	31	15	16	36	15	21	33	15	18	31	0.81		15	16	15
31 HOOVER	10	10		11	8		21	12	9		12	9	27	13	14	28	14	14	29	14	15	24	14	10	36	-9	0.3667	14	22	14
32 F D ROOSEVELT	24	21		25	22		2	28	26		28	25	2	31	29	1	32	31	1	32	31	2	32	30	2	3.97		30	28	35
33 TRUMAN	X	X		26	18		8	29	21		29	21	7	32	25	7	33	26	7	33	26	8	33	26	8	3.1		31	23	36
34 EISENHOWER	X	X		7	14		11	7	4		7	2	10	8	2	12	8	4	8	8	0	9	8	1	10	2.34		8	2	8
35 KENNEDY	X	X		X	X		13	30	17		30	16	13	33	20	10	34	24	10	35	25	15	35	20	12	2.29		33	21	38
36 L JOHNSON	X	X		X	X		10	33	23		33	21	14	36	22	15	37	22	13	38	25	12	38	26	15	2.21		36	21	42
37 NIXON	X	X		X	X		34	8	26		8	27	35	9	26	25	9	16	23	9	14	32	9	23	37	-21	-0.6774	9	28	9
38 FORD	X	X		X	X		24	14	10		14	9	24	15	9	27	16	11	32	16	16	27	16	11	29	1		16	13	16
39 CARTER	X	X		X	X		25	27	2		27	0	30	30	0	24	31	2	25	31	6	19	31	12	28	1.37		29	1	34
40 REAGAN	X	NR											20	3	17	22	3	19	20	3	17	26	3	23	26	1.42		3	23	3
41 G H W BUSH	X	X		X												18	10	8	31	10	21	22	10	12	25	1.45		10	15	10
42 CLINTON	X	X		X			X						X						16	34	18	23	34	11	21	1.58		32	11	37
43 G W BUSH	X			X			X						X			X			X			X	X							27
44 OBAMA	X			X			X						X			X			X			X	X							41
45 TRUMP	X			X			X						X			X			X			X	X							23

	SUM S48	SUM S62	M-B M82	SUM CT82	SIE SIE82	SUM SIE90	SUM SIE94	SUM RM96	SUM SCH96	REAL201
RR	215	253	357	351	408	463	489	490	444	
PER PRES:	7.17	7.91	9.65	9.49	10.2	11.29	11.927	11.95		11.1
OFF BY 5 OR LESS	15	14	15	14	16	11	15	13		14
OFF BY 10 OR MORE	11	10	14	13	15	18	19	22		19
NET AGREEMENT	4	4	1	1	1	-7	-4	-9		-5
NET AGR ADJUSTED	5.63	5.29	1.15	1.15	1.125	-7.68	-4.2857	-9.64		-5.3571
EXACT MATCHES WITH R-R	2	0	2	1	4	1	2	3		1

APPENDIX E PAGE 2

REAL RANKING COMPARED TO OTHER PRESIDENTIAL RANKINGS

2000–2005 polls

President	C-SPAN 2000	RR ADJUS	DELTA C-SPAN 2000 VS RR	WALL STREET JRNL 2000	RR ADJ	DELTA RR VS WSJ 2000	SIENA 2002	SNA 2002 RATING SCORE	RR ADJUS	DLTA SNA 2002 VS RR	WALL STREET JRNL 2005	RR ADJ	DELTA RR VS WSJ 2005
1 WASHINGTON	3	1	2		1	0	4	84.53	1	3		1	0
2 ADAMS	16	5	11		5	8	12	69.8	5	7		5	8
3 JEFFERSON	7	4	3		4	0	5	81.39	4	1		4	0
4 MADISON	18	36	18		34	19	9	72.71	37	28		35	18
5 MONROE	14	17	3		17	1	8	72.74	17	9		17	1
6 J Q ADAMS	19	18	1		18	2	17	66.6	18	1		18	7
7 JACKSON	13	39	26		37	31	13	69.73	40	27		38	28
8 VAN BUREN	30	30	0		28	5	24	57.9	31	7		29	2
9 W H HARRISON	37	23	14				36	48.98	23	13			
10 TYLER	36	29	7		27	7	37	48.78	30	7		28	7
11 POLK	12	6	6		6	4	11	70.5	6	5		6	3
12 TAYLOR	28	19	9		19	12	34	50.9	19	15		19	14
13 FILLMORE	35	27	8		25	10	38	48.74	28	10		26	10
14 PIERCE	39	41	2		39	2	39	44.21	42	3		40	2
15 BUCHANAN	41	40	1		38	1	41	39.85	41	0		39	1
16 LINCOLN	1	2	1		2	0	2	85.76	2	0		2	0
17 A JOHNSON	40	28	12		26	10	42	39.3	29	13		27	10
18 GRANT	33	25	8		23	9	35	50.23	26	9		24	5
19 HAYES	26	20	6		20	2	27	54.93	20	7		20	4
20 GARFIELD	29	22	7				33	52.14	22	11			
21 ARTHUR	32	11	21		11	15	30	53.7	11	19		11	15
22 CLEVELAND 1	17	24	7		22	10	20	61.93	24	4		22	1
23 B HARRISON	31	21	10		21	6	32	52.72	21	11		21	9
24 CLEVELAND 2	17	24	7		22	10	20	61.93	24	4		22	1
25 MCKINLEY	15	12	3		12	2	19	62.42	12	7		12	2
26 T ROOSEVELT	4	7	3		7	2	3	84.95	7	4		7	2
27 TAFT	24	13	11		13	6	21	59.86	13	8		13	7
28 WILSON	6	37	31		35	24	6	74.93	38	32		36	25
29 HARDING	38	26	12		24	13	40	42.91	27	13		25	14
30 COOLIDGE	27	15	12		15	10	29	54.21	15	14		15	8
31 HOOVER	34	14	20		14	15	31	53.17	14	17		14	17
32 F D ROOSEVELT	2	32	30		30	27	1	88.92	33	32		31	28
33 TRUMAN	5	33	28		31	24	7	73.19	34	27		32	25
34 EISENHOWER	9	8	1		8	1	10	71.3	8	2		8	0
35 KENNEDY	8	35	27		33	15	14	69.56	36	22		34	19
36 L JOHNSON	10	38	28		36	19	15	67.5	39	24		37	26
37 NIXON	25	9	16		9	24	26	55.99	9	17		9	14
38 FORD	23	16	7		16	12	28	54.46	16	12		16	8
39 CARTER	22	31	9		29	1	25	57.35	32	7		30	4
40 REAGAN	11	3	8		3	5	16	67.05	3	13		3	3
41 G H W BUSH	20	10	10		10	11	22	59.46	10	12		10	11
42 CLINTON	21	34	13		32	8	18	65.48	35	17		33	11
43 G W BUSH	X						23	58.56	25	2		23	4
44 OBAMA	X												
45 TRUMP	X												

2009–2015 polls

President	C-SPAN 2009	RR ADJUS	DLTA C-S 2009 VS RR	SIENA 2010	RR ADJ	DELTA RR VS SIENA 2010	USPC 2011	RR ADJ	DELTA RR VS USPC 2011	AMER POL SCI ASSN 2015	RR ADJ	DELTA RR VS APSA 2015
1 WASHINGTON	2	1	1	4	1	3	3	1	2	2	1	1
2 ADAMS	17	5	12	17	5	12	12	5	7	15	5	10
3 JEFFERSON	7	4	3	5	4	1	4	4	0	5	4	1
4 MADISON	20	37	17	6	37	31	14	35	21	13	37	24
5 MONROE	14	17	3	7	17	10	13	17	4	16	17	1
6 J Q ADAMS	19	18	1	19	18	20	20	18	2	22	18	4
7 JACKSON	13	40	27	14	41	27	9	38	29	9	41	32
8 VAN BUREN	31	31	0	23	31	8	27	29	6	25	31	6
9 W H HARRISON	39	23	16	35	23	12	NR			39	23	16
10 TYLER	35	30	5	37	30	7	37	28	9	36	30	6
11 POLK	12	6	6	12	6	13	16	6	10	19	6	13
12 TAYLOR	29	19	10	33	19	14	33	19	14	33	19	14
13 FILLMORE	37	28	9	38	28	10	35	26	9	37	28	9
14 PIERCE	40	42	2	40	43	3	39	40	1	40	43	3
15 BUCHANAN	42	41	1	42	42	0	40	39	1	43	42	1
16 LINCOLN	1	2	1	3	2	1	2	2	0	1	2	1
17 A JOHNSON	41	29	12	43	29	14	36	27	9	41	29	12
18 GRANT	23	26	3	26	26	0	29	24	5	28	26	2
19 HAYES	33	20	13	31	20	11	30	20	10	30	20	10
20 GARFIELD	28	22	6	27	22	5	NR			31	22	9
21 ARTHUR	32	11	21	25	11	14	32	11	21	32	11	21
22 CLEVELAND 1	21	24	3	20	24	4	21	24	1	23	24	1
23 B HARRISON	30	21	9	34	21	13	34	21	13	29	21	8
24 CLEVELAND 2	21	24	3	20	24	4	21	24	1	23	24	1
25 MCKINLEY	16	12	4	21	12	9	17	12	5	16	12	9
26 T ROOSEVELT	4	7	3	2	7	5	5	7	2	4	7	3
27 TAFT	24	13	11	24	13	11	25	13	12	20	13	7
28 WILSON	9	38	29	8	38	30	6	36	30	10	38	28
29 HARDING	38	27	11	41	27	14	38	25	13	42	27	15
30 COOLIDGE	26	15	11	29	15	14	28	15	13	27	15	12
31 HOOVER	34	14	20	36	14	22	26	14	12	38	14	24
32 F D ROOSEVELT	3	33	30	1	33	32	1	30	30	3	33	30
33 TRUMAN	5	34	29	9	34	25	7	32	25	6	34	28
34 EISENHOWER	8	8	0	10	8	2	10	8	2	7	8	1
35 KENNEDY	6	36	30	11	36	25	15	34	19	14	36	22
36 L JOHNSON	11	39	28	16	40	24	11	37	26	12	40	28
37 NIXON	27	9	18	30	9	21	23	9	14	34	9	25
38 FORD	22	16	6	28	16	12	24	16	8	24	16	8
39 CARTER	25	32	7	32	32	0	18	30	12	26	32	6
40 REAGAN	10	3	7	18	3	15	9	3	8	9	3	6
41 G H W BUSH	18	10	8	22	10	12	22	10	10	17	10	7
42 CLINTON	15	35	20	13	35	22	19	33	14	8	35	27
43 G W BUSH	36	25	11	39	25	14	31	23	8	35	25	10
44 OBAMA				15	39	24	X			18	39	21
45 TRUMP												

2017–2019 polls

President	C-SPAN 2017	RR ADJ	DELTA RR VS C-S 2017	AMER POL SCI ASSN 2018	RR ADJ	DELTA RR VS APSA 2018	IVAN ELAND 2014	RR ADJ	DELTA RR VS I ELAND	REAL RANKING FEB 5, 2019
1 WASHINGTON	2	1	1	2	1	1	7	1	6	1
2 ADAMS	19	5	14	14	5	9	22	5	17	5
3 JEFFERSON	7	4	3	5	4	1	26	4	22	4
4 MADISON	17	37	20	12	38	26	28	35	7	39
5 MONROE	13	17	4	18	17	1	25	17	8	17
6 J Q ADAMS	21	18	3	23	18	5	12	18	6	18
7 JACKSON	18	41	23	15	42	27	27	39	12	43
8 VAN BUREN	34	31	3	27	32	5	3	29	26	33
9 W H HARRISON	38	23	15	42	24	18	NR			24
10 TYLER	39	30	9	37	31	6	1	28	27	32
11 POLK	14	6	8	20	6	14	38	6	32	6
12 TAYLOR	31	19	12	35	19	16	13	19	6	19
13 FILLMORE	37	28	9	38	29	9	14	26	12	30
14 PIERCE	41	43	2	41	44	3	24	41	17	45
15 BUCHANAN	43	42	1	43	43	0	23	40	17	44
16 LINCOLN	1	2	1	1	2	1	29	2	27	2
17 A JOHNSON	42	29	13	40	30	10	17	27	10	31
18 GRANT	22	26	4	21	27	6	19	24	5	28
19 HAYES	32	20	12	29	20	9	4	20	16	20
20 GARFIELD	29	22	7	34	22	12	NR			22
21 ARTHUR	35	11	24	31	11	20	5	11	6	11
22 CLEVELAND 1	23	24	1	24	25	1	2	22	20	25
23 B HARRISON	30	21	9	32	21	11	15	21	6	21
24 CLEVELAND 2	23	24	1	24	25	1	2	22	20	26
25 MCKINLEY	16	12	4	19	12	7	39	12	27	12
26 T ROOSEVELT	4	7	3	4	7	3	21	7	14	7
27 TAFT	24	13	11	22	13	9	20	13	7	13
28 WILSON	11	38	27	11	39	28	41	36	5	40
29 HARDING	40	27	13	39	28	11	6	25	19	29
30 COOLIDGE	27	15	12	28	15	13	10	15	5	15
31 HOOVER	36	14	22	36	14	22	18	14	4	14
32 F D ROOSEVELT	3	33	30	3	34	31	31	31	0	35
33 TRUMAN	6	34	28	6	35	29	40	32	8	36
34 EISENHOWER	5	8	3	7	8	1	9	8	1	8
35 KENNEDY	8	36	28	16	37	21	36	34	2	38
36 L JOHNSON	10	40	30	10	41	31	32	38	6	42
37 NIXON	28	9	19	33	9	24	30	9	21	9
38 FORD	25	16	9	25	16	9	16	16	0	16
39 CARTER	26	32	6	26	33	7	8	30	22	34
40 REAGAN	9	3	6	9	3	6	35	3	32	3
41 G H W BUSH	20	10	10	17	10	7	33	10	23	10
42 CLINTON	15	35	20	13	36	23	11	33	22	37
43 G W BUSH	33	25	8	30	26	4	37	23	14	27
44 OBAMA	12	39	27	8	40	32	34	37	3	41
45 TRUMP	X			44	23	21				23

Summary

	C-S 2000	WSJ 00	SIE 02	WSJ 05	C-S 2009	SIE 10	USP C 11	APSA 15	C-S 17	APSA 18	IE14	REAL 2019
SUM RR	459	383	496		398	467	544	433	525	515	253	357
PER PRES:	11.19512	9.575	11.535	9.707317	10.86	12.36364	10.56098	11.93182	11.705	5.622222	8.5	
OFF BY 5 OR LESS	11	15	12	15	16	13	15	12	14	13	9	
OFF BY 10 OR MORE	19	19	22	20	20	27	20	21	21	21	23	
NET AGREEMENT	-8	-4	-10	-5	-4	-14	-5	-9	-7	-22	-14	
	-8.57143	-4.5	-10.47	-5.4878	-4.186	-14.3182	-5.4878	-9.20455	-7.159	-22	-27.39	
EXACT MATCHES WITH R-R	1	3	2	3	2	3	2	0	0	1	2	

APPENDIX E PAGE 3

REAL RANKING COMPARED TO OTHER PRESIDENTIAL RANKINGS

METHODOLOGY:

SCHLESINGER 1948 FROM WIKIPEDIA, FROM GARY M. MAXWELL IN JOURNAL OF AMERICAN HISTORY #57

SCHLESINGER 1962 FROM WIKIPEDIA, , DATA DERIVED FROM "OUR PRESIDENTS: A RATING BY 75 HISTORIANS" NEW YORK TIMES JULY 1962

MURRAY - BLESSING 1982 FROM WIKIPEDIA FROM Greatness in the Whte House: Rating the Presidents, from Washington Through Ronald Reagan by Robert K. Murray and Tim H. Blessing

CHICAGO TRIBUNE 1982 FROM WIKIPEDIA

FROM SIENA COLLEGE RESEASRCH INSTITUTE   U S PRESIDENTS STUDY   HISTORICAL RANKINGS

       SIENA 1982 PRESIDENTIAL RANKINGS BASED ON

       BACKGROUND, PARTY LEADERSHIP, COMMUNICATIONS, CONGREESSIONAL RELATIONSHIP, COURT APPOINTMENTS

       HANDLING ECONOMY, LUCK, COMPROMISES, RISK TAKING, EXEC APPOINTMENTS, OVERALL ABILITY, IMAGINATION, ACCOMPLISHMENTS DOMESTIC,

       INTEGRITY, EXEC ABILITY, FOREIGN POLICY ACCOMPLISHMENTS, LEADERDSHIP, INTELLIGENCE

       AVOIDING CRUCIAL MISTAKES,   WITH SOME WEIGHTING OF FACTORS

       SIENA 1990, 1994, 2002, 2010 PRESIDENTIAL RANKINGS BASED ON VARYING CRITERIA, SOMETIMES VALUES CHANGE

RIDINGS & MCIVER 1996 FROM WIKIPEDIA

SCHLESINGER '96: RATE BY VOTER: GREAT =4, NEAR GREAT=3. AVERAGE = 2, BELOW AVRAGE = -1, FAILURE = -2, D

       DIVIDE SUM BY # OF VOTERS   EXCEPT FAILURE IS GROSS TOTAL, NO DIVISION

       "RATING THE PRESIDENTS: WASHINGTON TO CLINTON" A.M. SCHLESINGER JR

       POLITICAL SCIENCE QUARTERLY, VOL 112 #2 SUMMER 1997

C-SPAN RANKINGS 2000,2009, 2017 FROM cx-span.org/presidentsurvey...

WSJ 2000 FROM WIKIPEDIA FROM FEDERALIST SOCIETY, //fedsoc.org/commentary/publications/rating...

WSJ 2005 presidential rankings FROM WIKIPEDIA from Wall Street Journal Monday September 12, 2005

USPC 2011 FROM WIKIPEDIA

AMERICAN POLITICAL SCIENCE ASSOCIATION 2015, 2018 FROM WIKIPEDIA

IVAN ELAND, RECARVING RUSHMORE: RANKING THE PRESIDENTS ON PEACE, PROSPERITY, AND LIBERTY (OAKLAND: INDEPENDENT INSTITUTE, 2014)

REAL RATING ADJUSTED TO MATCH POLL BEING COMPARED I.E. DELETE WH HARRISON, GARFIELD, ETC, SINGLE CLEVELAND

OFF BY 5 OR LESS =NUMBER OF RANKINGS BY POLL AND REAL RANKING THAT DISAGREE BY 5 OR LESS

OFF BY 10 OR MORE = NUMBER OF RANKINGS BY POLL AND REAL RANKING THAT DISAGREE BY 10 OR MORE

NET AGREEMENT = NUMBER OFF BY 5 OR LESS MINUS NUMBER OFF BY 10 OR MORE POSITIVE GOOD, NEGATIVE BAD

NET AGR ADJUSTED = NET AGREEMENT FACTORED FOR NUMBER OF PRESIDENTS EVALUATED

EXACT MATCHES WITH R-R = NUMBER OF PRESIDENTS WITH SAME RANKING FOR POLL AND REAL RANKING

APPENDIX F

CHANGES IN MAINSTREAM PRESIDENTIAL RANKINGS VS. TIME

REAL RANKING OF THE PRESIDENTS
APPENDIX F 20200116

REVISED AND ADJUSTED

CLEVELAND ONE RANKING, DUPLICATED FOR 1ST & 2ND TERMS

	INVERT SCHLESINGER SR 1948	INVERT SCHLESINGER 1962	INVERT M-B 1982	INVERT CHICAGO TRIBUNE 1982	INVERT SIENA 1982	INVERT SIENA 1990	INVERT SIENA 1994	INVERT RIDINGS & MCIVER 1996	INVERT RANK SCHLESINGER 1996	INVERT C-SPAN 2000	INVEERT WALL STREET JRNL 2000	INVERT SIENA 2002	INVERET WALL STREET JRNL 2005	INVERT C-SPAN 2009	INVERT SIENA 2010	INVERT USPC 2011	INVERT AMER POL SCI ASSN 2015	INVERT C-SPAN 2017	INVERT AMER POL SCI ASSN 2018	NET CHANGE: LAST - FIRST	NET CHANGE: LAST 5 - FIRST 5	NET: LAST UP TO 8 - FIRST UP TO 8	
	1	2	3	4	5	6	7	8	9		9	8	7	6	5	4	3	2	1				
4	1	2	3	4	5	6	7	8	9	10	11	12	13	14	15	16	17	18	19				
1 WASHINGTON	43	43	42	43	41	41	41	42	43	42	44	41	44	43	41	42	43	43	43	0	0	0.556	WASHINGTON
2 ADAMS	36	35	36	30	37	31	33	31	34	29	32	33	32	28	28	33	30	26	31	-5	-5.2	-3.333	ADAMS
3 JEFFERSON	40	40	41	40	43	42	40	41	41	38	41	40	41	38	40	41	40	38	40	0	-1	-1.000	JEFFERSON
4 MADISON	31	33	31	28	33	37	36	35	27	27	30	36	28	25	39	31	32	28	33	2	1.4	-1.000	MADISON
5 MONROE	33	27	30	29	29	34	30	32	29	31	29	37	29	31	38	32	29	32	27	-6	2	1.222	MONROE
6 J Q ADAMS	34	32	29	26	28	29	28	27	26	26	25	28	20	26	26	25	23	24	22	-12	-5.8	-4.444	J Q ADAMS
7 JACKSON	39	39	38	38	36	36	34	37	40	32	39	32	35	32	31	36	36	27	30	-9	-6	-4.333	JACKSON
8 VAN BUREN	30	28	25	27	24	24	23	24	23	15	22	21	18	14	22	18	20	11	18	-12	-9	-7.111	VAN BUREN
9 W H HARRISON					20	10	17	10	9	8	12	9	8	6	10	9	6	7	3	-17	-6.2	-5.286	W H HARRISON
10 TYLER	23	20	17	17	13	12	11	11	12	9	11	8	10	10	8	8	9	6	8	-15	-10.2	-6.444	TYLER
11 POLK	35	37	33	35	34	32	31	34	36	33	35	34	36	33	33	29	26	31	25	-10	-6	-2.778	POLK
12 TAYLOR	20	21	18	19	14	11	12	16	15	17	14	11	12	16	12	12	12	14	10	-10	-6.4	-3.667	TAYLOR
13 FILLMORE	21	19	16	14	16	13	10	9	13	10	10	7	9	8	7	10	8	8	7	-14	-9.2	-6.333	FILLMORE
14 PIERCE	18	17	14	12	11	9	8	8	11	6	7	6	7	5	5	6	5	4	4	-14	-9.6	-6.556	PIERCE
15 BUCHANAN	19	16	12	11	7	7	6	5	6	4	6	4	5	3	3	5	2	2	2	-17	-10.2	-6.333	BUCHANAN
16 LINCOLN	44	44	44	44	42	43	43	44	44	44	43	43	43	44	42	43	44	44	44	0	-0.2	-0.222	LINCOLN
17 A JOHNSON	26	22	13	15	9	6	5	6	7	5	9	3	8	4	2	9	4	3	5	-21	-12.4	-6.889	A JOHNSON
18 GRANT	17	15	10	13	8	8	7	7	10	12	13	10	16	22	19	16	17	23	24	7	7.2	7.222	GRANT
19 HAYES	32	31	23	23	19	22	21	20	21	19	23	18	21	12	14	15	15	13	16	-16	-11	-7.222	HAYES
20 GARFIELD					22	15	19	15	17	16	15	12	19	17	18	17	14	16	11	-11	-2.4	-1.000	GARFIELD
21 ARTHUR	28	24	22	21	23	19	18	17	18	13	19	15	19	13	20	13	13	10	14	-14	-9.6	-6.000	ARTHUR
22 CLEVELAND 1	37	34	28	32	30	28	26	29	32	28	33	25	33	24	25	24	22	22	21	-16	-9.4	-5.222	CLEVELAND 1
23 B HARRISON	24	25	19	20	17	16	15	14	25	14	18	13	15	15	11	11	16	15	13	-11	-7.8	-5.333	B HARRISON
24 CLEVELAND 2	37	34	28	32	30	28	26	29	32	28	33	25	33	24	25	24	22	22	21	-16	-9.4	-5.222	CLEVELAND 2
25 MCKINLEY	27	30	27	34	27	26	27	28	28	30	31	26	31	29	24	28	24	29	26	-1	-2.8	-0.667	MCKINLEY
26 T ROOSEVELT	38	38	40	41	40	40	42	40	39	41	40	42	40	41	43	40	41	41	41	3	1.8	1.222	T ROOSEVELT
27 TAFT	29	29	26	25	26	25	24	25	22	21	26	24	25	21	21	20	25	21	23	-6	-5	-2.778	TAFT
28 WILSON	41	41	39	39	39	39	39	39	38	39	34	39	34	36	37	39	35	34	34	-7	-4	-3.556	WILSON
29 HARDING	16	14	9	9	6	5	4	4	5	7	7	5	6	7	4	7	3	5	6	-10	-5.8	-2.444	HARDING
30 COOLIDGE	22	18	15	16	12	14	9	12	14	18	20	16	22	19	16	17	18	18	17	-5	0.6	3.444	COOLIDGE
31 HOOVER	25	26	24	24	18	17	16	21	9	11	16	14	14	11	9	19	7	9	9	-16	-12.8	-8.000	HOOVER
32 F D ROOSEVELT	42	42	43	42	44	44	44	43	43	43	42	44	42	42	44	44	42	42	42	0	0.2	-0.333	F D ROOSEVELT
33 TRUMAN		37	37	37	38	38	38	38	37	40	38	38	38	40	36	38	39	39	39	2	0.8	0.556	TRUMAN
34 EISENHOWER		24	34	36	35	33	37	36	35	36	36	35	37	37	35	35	38	40	38	14	4.8	2.778	EISENHOWER
35 KENNEDY			32	31	32	35	35	30	33	37	27	31	30	39	34	30	31	37	29	-3	-0.8	-0.500	KENNEDY
36 L JOHNSON			35	33	31	30	32	33	30	35	28	30	27	34	29	34	33	35	35	0	1	-0.250	L JOHNSON
37 NIXON			11	10	10	20	22	13	8	20	12	19	13	18	15	22	11	17	12	1	0.8	1.625	NIXON
38 FORD			21	22	21	18	13	18	16	22	17	17	17	23	17	21	21	20	20	-1	0.8	0.625	FORD
39 CARTER			20	18	15	21	20	26	17	23	15	20	11	20	13	27	19	19	19	-1	0.6	-1.500	CARTER
40 REAGAN					20	19	25	19	19	34	37	29	39	35	27	37	34	36	36	16	13.6	10.143	REAGAN
41 G H W BUSH						23	14	23	20	25	24	23	24	27	23	23	28	25	28	5	4.4	3.714	G H W BUSH
42 CLINTON							29	22	24	24	21	27	23	30	32	26	37	30	32	3	7.4	6.667	CLINTON
43 G W BUSH												22	26	9	6	14	10	12	15	-7 NR		-3.000	G W BUSH
44 OBAMA															30		27	33	37	7 NR		6.500	OBAMA
45 TRUMP																			1 NR	NR	NR		TRUMP

	NET CHANGE: LAST - FIRST	NET CHANGE: LAST 5 - FIRST 5	NET: LAST UP TO 8 - FIRST UP TO 8
PLUS	10	15	13
MINUS	29	26	31
ZERO	5	1	0
TROTAL	44	42	44

NOTE: CLEVELAND COUNTED TWICE BUT SAME RANKING USED BOTH TIMES

COMPARING FIRST AND LAST RANKING: ONLY INCLUDES 2 RANKINGS	4 DEMOCRATS IMPROVE 13 DEMOCRATS DROP 3 DEMOCRATS STAY SAME	6 REPUBLICANS IMPROVE 16 REPUBLICANS DROP 2 REPUBLICANS STAY SAME
COMPARING FIRST HALF TO LAST HALF INCLUDES ALL RANKINGS EXCEPT FOR MIDDLE ONE	4 DEMOCRATS IMPROVE 16 DEMOCRATS DROP	9 REPUBLICANS IMPROVE 15 REPUBLICANS DROP
COMPARING FIRST 5 TO LAST 5 42 PRESIDENTS ONLY	7 DEMOCRATS IMPROVE 12 DEMOCRATS DROP 0 DEMOCRATS STAY SAME	8 REPUBLICANS IMPROVE 14 REPUBLICANS DROP 1 REPUBLICANS STAY SAME

INDEX

land grants, 41, 90, 123

Latin America, 50, 69, 112

lavender, 6, 7, 8

lawyer, 41, 62

League of Nations, 63, 89, 111, 113

Lebanon, 43, 54

liberal, 4, 5, 6, 8, 9, 14, 15, 22, 23, 28,
42, 45, 54, 55, 80, 88, 94, 103, 108,
109, 113, 130, 140, 143, 160, 163

libertarian, x, 28, 29, 30, 33, 83, 143,
160, 163, 169

Lincoln, Abraham, xiii, 11, 12, 19, 28,
29, 37, 39-42, 45, 68, 70, 72, 73, 91,
92, 98, 110, 126, 131, 132, 133, 138,
139, 144, 146, 148, 150, 152, 153,
154, 155, 156, 157, 158, 159, 160,
161, 162,

Lindbergh, Charles, 97

Lindgren, James, 156

lobbyists, 28

Locofoco, 33

Louisiana, 7, 19, 39, 40

Louisiana Purchase, 9, 10, 39, 46, 50

Louisiana Territory, 45

MacArthur, Douglas, 102

Madison, James, xiii, 1, 9, 10, 110-111,
126, 133, 144, 146, 148, 150, 152,
155, 157, 158, 159, 161

Maine, 7, 93, 95

mainstream, 28, 29, 83, 117, 143, 144,
145, 156, 157, 160, 163, 169, 174

Manifest Destiny, 48

Mariel Boatlift, 96

Marshall Plan, 102

Marshall, John, 47, 48, 120

Maryland, xi, 5, 7, 40

Mason-Dixon Line, 111

Massachusetts, xi, 4, 7, 42

McCarthy Era, 42

McIver, Stuart B., 154

McKinley, William, xiii, 20, 50, 61-62,
84, 126, 132, 133, 136, 141, 144,
146, 148, 150, 152, 153, 155, 157,
158, 159, 161

Medicare, 43, 103, 105

Mexican War, 11, 49, 71, 72, 87, 93

Mexico, 28, 58, 78, 123

Michigan, 7, 10, 31, 79

middle class, 10, 14, 21, 28, 33, 35, 108,
147

Middle East, 54, 86, 96

Middle West, 41

middle-of-the-road, 53, 55

Midwest, 40, 80

military-industrial complex,

militia,

millenials,

miners,

minimum wage,

Minnesota,

Missouri, 7, 40, 101

Mississippi, 7, 19, 39, 109

Mississippi River Basin, 45

Missouri Compromise, 124

Monroe Doctrine, 51

Monroe, James, xiii, 1, 10, 23, 68-70,
126, 133, 135, 144, 145, 146, 148,
150, 152, 155, 157, 158, 159, 161

Montana, x, 7

Moon, 56, 108

Morgan, J.P., 51

pet banks, 119

Philippines, 61, 62

Pierce, Franklin, 1, 11, 117, 123-125, 126, 144, 145, 146, 148, 151, 152, 153, 154, 155, 157, 158, 159, 161

pink, 6-8

Poland, viii, 13, 102

political parties, xii, 30, 32, 33, 37, 53, 118

Polk, James K., 11, 28, 48-50, 72, 93, 126, 144, 146, 148, 150, 151, 152, 153, 155, 157, 158, 159, 161

popular vote, x-xii, 2, 12, 19-21, 23, 25, 26, 30, 33, 35, 39, 67, 71, 79, 80, 88, 90, 97, 101, 108, 129, 130-133, 135, 137, 138, 139, 140, 141, 163, 165

popularity, 14, 15, 22, 23, 27, 28, 29, 55, 57, 66, 67, 69, 96, 101, 109, 110, 125, 127, 129, 135, 143, 153, 163,

populism, 12

pork-barrel, 60

Potomac River, 38

Potsdam Conference, 13

powers per constitution, president, ix

Preamble, vii

President of the Senate, 25

presidential succession, 60

Press, the, 2, 129

prime minister, xi, 104,

Princeton University, 111, 154

progressive, 12, 20, 21, 33, 50, 52, 63, 66, 111, 112, 129, 136, 139

Progressive Party, 33, 66, 139

Progressivism, 12, 111, 136

proletariat, 10, 36

protective tariff, 59, 61, 72, 76

protocols, 37

public works, 32, 64

Puerto Rico, 61

Pullman Strike, 84

pundits, 30, 55

purple, xi, 4, 6, 7, 8

race problem, 14

radio, 98

railroads, 12, 32, 41, 50, 51, 53, 71, 81, 112, 123

Randolph, John, 4

rank, 26

Reagan Revolution, 28

Reagan, Ronald, 17, 22, 23, 37 42-44, 58, 96, 97, 133, 136, 141, 146, 148, 150, 155, 162

Real Ranking, 27-30, 83, 85, 126, 133, 143, 144, 146, 147, 148, 149, 151, 152, 153, 154, 155, 156, 157, 158, 160, 163, 164, 169, 171, 172, 173

recession, 22, 67, 68, 86, 96, 100, 114

Reconstruction, 19, 72, 74, 81,87, 92

red , xi

"Republican", 9, 17, 18, 31, 32, 37, 45, 68, 70, 110, 132,

Republicans, x, xiii, 1, 2, 10-12, 15, 17, 18, 20-22, 31-32, 34, 35, 39, 41, 53, 54, 61, 62, 68, 74, 76, 80, 81, 84, 88, 103, 114, 117, 132, 133, 141, 149, 153, 156, 158, 160,

revolution, 28, 31, 47, 51, 111, 119

Rhode Island, vii, xi, 3, 7, 35, 38, 131

rice, 5

Ridings, William J. Jr, 154

Ripon, Wisconsin, 31

9 781648 049446